Sunset

Tax$aver
Outside Sales

By Jay Knepp, CPA
Tax Specialist

Lane Publishing Co.　■　**Menlo Park, California**

Edited by Fran Feldman
Coordinating Editor: Linda Selden
Design: Brooklyn Graphic
Cover Design: Design Systems Group

Sunset Books
 Editor: David E. Clark
 Managing Editor: Elizabeth L. Hogan

First printing November 1987

From Coopers & Lybrand

We have reviewed *Outside Sales Tax$aver* for accuracy in its description of federal income tax law.

Based on our interpretation of the Internal Revenue Code (including 1986 amendments) and its regulations, public rulings, and court decisions, we believe that *Tax$aver* accurately describes and interprets the applicable provisions of the law. Any taxpayer who follows the guidance of *Tax$aver* will have appropriate documentation to support his or her business-related deductions.

However, it is important to recognize that federal income tax laws and application of the Internal Revenue Service code and regulations are often a matter of interpretation. As a result, an Internal Revenue Service agent examining a taxpayer's return may disagree with the treatment of certain items of income and deductions as covered in this book. Because tax laws are continually subject to change by legislation, Internal Revenue Service regulations, public rulings, and court decisions, we cannot guarantee that a position taken by a taxpayer based on information in this book will not be successfully challenged by the Internal Revenue Service. In addition, individual facts and circumstances may result in an outcome different from that anticipated.

In view of the complexities of the tax laws and varying interpretations, taxpayers should not rely solely on the advice contained in *Tax$aver*, but should use it in conjunction with advice from their own tax advisor.

(Coopers & Lybrand is an international accounting firm with 98 offices in the United States.)

August 1987

Table of Contents

What *Tax$aver* Can Do for You

If you're an outside salesperson, whether you're employed or self-employed, you likely incur many deductible business expenses, most of which are subject to strict substantiation requirements. If you're concerned about those requirements as well as numerous changes in recent tax law, then *Outside Sales Tax$aver* is for you. It's a unique combination of tax advice and information together with a systematic record-keeping system designed to give the IRS the records and documentation it demands—and, in some cases, even more.

This book, specifically created with outside salespeople in mind, is designed for *you*, not for a tax specialist. It contains tax information on the situations you might encounter and tells you what to deduct, how to keep required records easily and simply, and how to prove your claims should you be audited.

Above all, the book helps you claim and prove every deduction you deserve—a goal of all taxpayers.

Deducting Outside Sales Expenses

Outside salespeople who use their car for business are entitled to deductions for their expenses. The same is true for away-from-home, travel, and entertainment expenses, which for outside salespeople usually are considerable. And if you use your home for business, such as for the storage of inventory or for an office and you can meet the strict rules and tests, other deductions may be available. In addition, you need to know about the deductibility of business gifts and educational, job-hunting, and moving expenses.

How you claim your deductions depends on whether you're an employee or self-employed. In the past, all outside salespeople could deduct their business expenses even if they didn't itemize. Under the new tax law, however, outside salespeople who are employees are now treated the same as all other employees—their unreimbursed expenses are deductible only as a miscellaneous itemized deduction on Schedule A and only for the amount the total of all such deductions exceeds 2% of their adjusted gross income. The self-employed, however, can deduct their unreimbursed business expenses, provided they meet the necessary tests and have adequate substantiation.

If you're presently employed and would like to avoid the adverse effects of the tax law changes, you may want to consider changing your status to self-employed. The options available to you and the criteria you need are fully explained.

The Importance of Good Records

Good records will help you prove not only the amount and type but also the nature of each income item or expenditure, essential for determining whether or not it's valid. With this book, you'll be armed both with tax knowledge and with excellent records for your sales activities. Together with receipts and other evidence, those records will help you substantiate all your claims.

Permanent annual records. The tax information and forms in this book are designed for one year's use. The reasons for this are simple and logical. Tax laws change constantly and starting a new book

each year enables you to keep current with developments and changes in tax laws. It reduces the chance you'll waste time and energy keeping records that are no longer required, or fail to meet some new requirement, which could prove costly. Also, with a permanent annual record, you'll always be prepared in the event of an audit.

Keeping abreast of tax law. Laws and regulations pertaining to travel and entertainment and to assets used for both business and personal purposes change rapidly. In addition, court decisions are continually influencing and reinterpreting tax law. Because many areas in tax law are simply too complex for the average taxpayer, it's always wise to consult a competent professional tax advisor about any situation that concerns you. For this reason, we've included a section to help you choose a tax advisor.

Tax terms. Baffled by the complicated terms used by the IRS in its tax forms and publications? In order to comply with all the regulations, it's essential to understand and speak their language. For definitions of the most commonly used terms, consult the glossary beginning on page 140. ■

Records & Rules

Record-keeping & Substantiation Requirements

Whether you're preparing your own tax return, turning your records over to a professional tax advisor, or facing an audit by the IRS, complete tax records maintained in an orderly, organized fashion are essential in order to substantiate your claims. Since outside salespeople incur frequent expenses for travel and entertainment, this substantiation becomes even more critical.

It's no secret that many taxpayers regard this work as tedious and unpleasant. But once you know what constitutes good records and how to keep them, and you understand how to use the specially designed forms in this book (all of which meet current IRS record-keeping requirements), you can make the tough IRS rules work *for* you, not against you.

Requirements for deductibility. In order to deduct an expenditure as a business expense, it must be directly related to a trade or business you conduct, it can't be an expense that should be capitalized (depreciated or written off over more than a year), and it must be ordinary and necessary in carrying on the trade or business, as well as reasonable in amount.

An *ordinary* expense is one that's customary or usual for taxpayers in similar trades or businesses. A *necessary* expense should be appropriate and helpful in the performance, promotion, or furtherance of your trade or business.

What are adequate records? The IRS does not require you to keep records in any particular form or by any special method. They say only that you must have adequate records and sufficient evidence which, in combination, can prove each element—*amount, time, place,* and *business purpose*—of an expenditure.

Receipts are ordinarily the best way to prove the amount of each separate expense. The only way you can prove the other elements is to write down the information either directly on the receipt or in a record book such as this one.

Entertainment expenses require a fifth element of proof—*business relationship.*

The IRS will deny any deductions for expenses if they appear to be lavish or extravagant, or if they're approximations. Business expenses must be related to business and properly substantiated, or your deductions may be disallowed.

These records should be permanent, accurate, complete, and supported by any documents that clearly establish the nature and intent of each expense. Remember, however, that any record or evidence is not the sole determinant of deductibility. The facts and circumstances of each case will often dictate the final tax result.

How elaborate your records need to be depends on your individual situation. However, entries on a desk calendar or canceled checks alone are not usually considered as proper proof when unsupported by other documentary evidence.

When to make entries. The IRS is emphatic that records written at or near the time the expense occurs and supported by sufficient documentary evidence are much more credible than oral evidence or evidence reconstructed later.

According to temporary IRS regulations now in effect, log entries for auto and computer use do not have to be contemporaneous, but the rules do state that "a log maintained on a weekly basis, which accounts for use during the week, shall be considered a record made at or near the time of such use." This regulation, an important development, means you can accumulate your receipts and notes and make entries *once* a week. Other expenses can be recorded less frequently; a good time is when you reconcile your bank account each month.

Tax$aver Tip. *An excellent way for people in outside sales to keep track of all expenses and uses, regardless of how they're paid, is to use a portable tape recorder (deductible as a business expense). You can then tape-record your activities and expenses during the week and enter all the information in this book the following week. It's a good idea to initial and date your entries.*

How to keep good records. This book provides all the specific instructions and forms you'll need for recording your expenses. Don't rely on memory—it's easy to forget the amount or reason for expenses (especially if they're incidental). Here are some additional hints:

- Always pay by check or credit card if possible, since you're instantly creating a useful record.
- Always ask for a receipt, especially when paying cash, and keep all receipts on file.
- When you can't get a receipt for a cash payment, record and explain the payment in your records as soon as possible.
- Though most expenses should be recorded separately, incidental expenses can be totaled by categories. For these you can make *one* entry for the entire day.

Accounting periods and methods. Most taxpayers are required to file their returns based on the calendar year, using the cash basis method of accounting. This means you report income when it's actually received, credited to your account, or made available to you on demand. Expenses, with few exceptions, are deducted in the year they're ac-

tually paid. Expenses charged on a credit card are deductible when charged.

How long to retain records. All logs, checkbooks, canceled checks, receipts, and tax returns should be retained for at least 3 years from the date of filing, the usual length of time the IRS may select a return for audit. However, if it's found that some income was not reported and such income is greater than 25% of what was reported, the period available for audit is 6 years after the return was filed. And the IRS can go back to *any* year when no return is filed, a return is false or fraudulent, or criminal activity is suspected.

We recommend that you keep canceled checks and other evidence for 6 years. The following records should be retained *indefinitely*:

1. Copies of all tax returns previously filed
2. Records that relate to the basis of all property owned, depreciated, sold, or exchanged
3. Business or investment property records required to figure the amount of depreciation or investment tax credit recapture due to sale or disposition of the property before the end of its estimated recovery period

4. Records to prove the cost and ownership of property in the event of a casualty loss or theft

You'll also need records from previous years if you file a claim for a refund for taxes you've overpaid, if you need to amend a previous year's return, or if changes in tax law entitle you to benefits only on the basis of previous years' records. Often, records can also be helpful to the executor of your estate.

If a previous year's return is lost or misplaced, you can get a copy from the IRS. Ask for Form 4506—Request for Copy of Tax Form.

Lastly, secure all records relating to a specific tax year in an envelope and store it in a safe place. Think of these records as tax insurance.

Penalties. The following penalties for noncompliance with IRS regulations will be assessed unless you can prove that your failure was due to reasonable cause, not willful neglect:

1. Failure to file: 5% for each month or portion thereof, not to exceed 25% of the tax, with a minimum penalty of the lesser of $100 or 100% of the tax due if not filed within 60 days

2. Failure to pay tax: ½% (in some cases 1%) of the unpaid tax per month or portion thereof, not to exceed 25% of the tax

3. Underpayment of tax due to negligence or intentional disregard of regulations: 5% of the entire underpayment, interest, and an added penalty equal to 50% of the interest due on the underpayment (doesn't apply to any portion subject to a fraud penalty)

4. Substantial understatement of liability: 25% of the understatement, which is considered substantial when it exceeds the greater of $5,000 or 10% of the correct tax ($10,000 for most corporations)

5. Fraud: 75% for any underpayment due to fraud on returns due after 1986, plus 50% of the interest payable on the underpayment

Finally, criminal *and* civil penalties are assessed when a taxpayer intentionally doesn't pay taxes, intentionally files a false return, or files no return at all. ■

Employee or Independent Contractor

Whether certain individuals are employees or independent contractors has been a controversial issue for many years. Both Congress and the IRS have issued a never-ending string of rulings, procedures, noncode provisions, and amendments in an attempt to clarify the situation. None of this has made the classification any easier, as there still is no single rule or test you can use to make the determination. Instead, decisions are made on a case-by-case basis after careful consideration of all the facts and circumstances.

The issue is very important to the IRS because employers have the responsibility to withhold from the income of their employees federal income, social security, and unemployment taxes, as well as to file payroll returns and W-2 statements for their employees. Moreover, employers are subject to penalties for not paying those taxes.

The issue has taken on greater importance since the passage of the Tax Reform Act of 1986.

Now, outside salespeople who are employees can deduct business expenses that exceed reimbursements only as a miscellaneous itemized deduction subject to the 2% of adjusted gross income limitation. Therefore, many employees may want to try to change their status to self-employed independent contractor in order to be able to deduct their expenses without limitation.

What's an employee? Generally, the relationship of employer and employee exists when the employer has the right to control and direct the employee, not only as to the result to be achieved but also as to the means employed by the employee to achieve the desired result. It's not necessary that the employer actually control the way the work is done, only that the employer has the *right* to do so. Many courts consider this right-to-control test the single most important factor in determining the status of the worker.

Here are some other factors indicating an employer/employee relationship:

1. The employer can terminate the person without cause.
2. The employer provides the worker with tools, supplies, or a place to work.
3. The individual receives benefits normally associated with employees, such as sick leave or paid vacation days.
4. The person is paid on an hourly or salary basis.
5. The person's hours are defined by the employer.
6. The individual works solely for the employer.

When an employer/employee relationship exists, it's of no consequence that the parties decide to designate an employee as a partner or independent contractor. It also doesn't matter how payments for compensation are figured, what they're called, or how much time the person works.

In two situations having to do with sales, the law says that people not considered employees for federal income tax withholding purposes *are* included as employees as far as withholding of social security taxes is concerned. One is a full-time life insurance sales agent who works primarily for one life insurance company. The other is a full-time traveling salesperson who obtains orders for an employer or customer for merchandise for resale or for supplies used in business operations. The work performed must be the salesperson's principal business activity.

What's an independent contractor? An independent contractor is a person subject to the control and direction of another merely as to the *result* of work to be accomplished, not the means and methods of doing so.

If any of the following factors are present, the indication is that the person is an independent contractor:

1. The individual is free to work for others.
2. The person is engaged in a distinct trade or business.
3. The person is paid on a commission basis.
4. The person determines the hours worked.

A statutory nonemployee category exists which allows direct sellers and real estate agents to be treated as self-employed for federal income tax and employment tax purposes. To qualify, substantially all your compensation must be directly related to sales or other output rather than to the amount of hours worked, and your services must be based on a written contract explicitly providing that you won't be treated as an employee for federal tax purposes.

Here are a few additional guidelines the IRS uses that favorably indicate independent contractor status:

1. A business that advertises its services, uses a business name listed in telephone directories, maintains an office, and has obtained any necessary licenses to conduct business

2. A person who can't be fired as long as a result which meets contract specifications is produced

3. A worker who has the right to delegate and bring in others to do their work

4. A significant investment made in the facilities needed for doing the work (other than for transportation)

5. Industry custom as to control ordinarily exercised and expertise required

Request for IRS ruling. If you want to be sure of your status, you can request a binding ruling by supplying all the information asked for on Form SS-8—Information for Use in Determining

Whether a Worker is an Employee for Purposes of Federal Employment Taxes and Income Tax Withholding.

Tax$aver Tip. *To help prove your status as an independent contractor, obtain a policy statement from companies you represent detailing your status.* ■

Income, Taxes & Reimbursements

Income received from any source is taxable, unless specifically excluded by provisions of the Internal Revenue Code or other federal law. If you're an employee, most types of income you earn will be reported annually to the IRS and to you on Form W-2—Wage and Tax Statement.

If you're self-employed, you should receive a Form 1099—MISC (for Miscellaneous Income) from everyone who paid you commissions, reimbursements of expenses, or any other type of income. A copy of this form is also sent to the IRS. You're required to keep accurate records of all income you receive, especially if it's not subject to withholding.

Employee Income

If you're an employee, your income includes all commissions, salaries, and wages earned, as well as other types of compensation you receive, such as bonuses and some fringe benefits.

The doctrine of constructive receipt. Taxpayers who use the cash basis method of accounting generally report income when it's received, rather than when it's earned. An exception to this rule is when you've *constructively received* income, that is, you have the right to draw on the income without having actual physical possession of the funds. Such income must be included in total income in the year of constructive receipt, not when actually received, provided that the income is credited to your account without restriction and is under your immediate control and disposition.

The most common example is a check either available to you or received by you just before the end of the tax year. Unless it was mailed so that it couldn't possibly reach you or you could not otherwise get the funds before the end of the year, you're treated as having received it in the earlier year, even if you didn't deposit the check until the next year. Commissions credited to your account are not considered as constructively received if the payer doesn't have sufficient funds to cover them.

Advance commissions. Advances you receive against commissions not yet earned are includible in gross income in the year the advances are received, unless there's an agreement that there's personal liability for repayment. If you repay unearned commissions in the same tax year, you simply reduce your income by the amount of the repayment. If you repay in a later tax year and the amount is $3,000 or less, you can claim it only as an itemized deduction on Schedule A, Form 1040. Such a deduction, referred to as a claim of right, is not subject to the 2% of adjusted gross income limitation.

If the repayment is over $3,000, however, figure your tax two different ways and use the one that results in the lower tax. The first method is to claim the repayment as an adjustment to taxable income in the year of repayment and then compute your tax. The second method is to figure the current year's tax without claiming the deduction. Then figure how much additional tax you paid in the earlier year because you included the amount later repaid and subtract the additional tax from the current year's tax. If this results in a lower tax than under the first method, claim a credit on page 2 of Form 1040 and label it "IRC 1341 credit" (the applicable code section). This method allows you the benefit even though you're not able to itemize.

The repayment rules do not apply to sales returns and allowances and to similar items resulting from sales to customers in the ordinary course of business, nor do the rules apply to bad debt deductions. If an advance is later canceled by your employer and treated and deducted as compensation paid, it's then considered taxable income. And if advances are customarily forgiven even if you're legally obligated to pay, it's income in the year of receipt.

If you receive minimum advances and can retain them regardless of the amount of commissions earned, the advances are income in the year received when any further commissions are withheld until they exceed the minimum. Amounts withheld from earned commissions in a later year to make up for this difference are not income.

If you use the accrual method of accounting and receive payments for services to be performed before the end of the next tax year, you can include the amounts in income as you earn them.

Bonuses, awards, and prizes. Payments to you for outstanding work, such as meeting sales goals, are income that should be included on your Form W-2. The fair market value of goods or services you receive, such as prize points redeemable for merchandise, is included in income in the year made available to you, not when used. You don't have to include in income a prize you refuse to accept or one that's merely promised.

Property as bargain purchases. If as compensation for services, you're allowed to buy property from your employer at less than fair market value, you must include in income as extra wages the excess of the fair market value over the purchase price.

Other taxable compensation. Here's a brief list of various transactions that are considered taxable income to you:

- Christmas gifts in cash, certificates, or anything easily exchangeable for cash
- Educational costs paid by your employer for courses that are not job-related (unless there's a written educational assistance plan)
- Moving expense allowance or reimbursements
- Payments by your employer for a *nonqualified* stock bonus, pension, profit-sharing, annuity, or bond purchase plan, unless your interest is subject to vesting, and for a *qualified* plan actually distributed or made available to you
- Payments by your employer for any type of personal expenses, such as commuting costs
- Payments by agreement for social security taxes not actually deducted from gross pay
- Sick or injury pay even if paid by others, provided the plan was paid for by your employer
- Settlements or judgments for back pay or unpaid life and health insurance premiums
- Severance pay for canceling an employment contract
- Vacation fund amounts paid to you

Fringe benefits. The value of some fringe benefits you receive from an employer must be included in income unless specifically excluded under the law. The taxable amount is the fair market value of the benefit, less any portion paid by you or excluded

17

by law. Taxable fringe benefits include the following:

- Educational assistance paid by your employer if the amount exceeds $5,250
- Executive health programs provided at resorts or athletic clubs
- Golden parachute payments (where your employer agrees to pay extra compensation if control or ownership of the business changes)
- Group-term life insurance coverage that exceeds $50,000 (the amount of the premiums paid by your employer less any part you pay)
- Meal allowances and reimbursements as added compensation on Form W-2
- Note received in payment of services (but not if it's security for payment)
- Unemployment compensation received under a federal or state program
- Value of personal use of an employer-provided car (see page 35), aircraft, computer, vacation trip, country club membership, travel, or entertainment

The following fringe benefits (if they qualify) are exempt from tax:

- Certain services sold to customers that are provided to employees and their families at no substantial added cost to your employer
- Discounts granted to employees and their families if they don't exceed 20% or the gross profit percentage of the customer price
- De minimis benefits provided occasionally that are too minimal to account for
- Working condition fringe provided by your employer but which you could claim as an employee business expense deduction if you had paid for it yourself

The first three items can't be excluded if they're available *only* to officers, owners, or highly paid employees.

Self-employment Income

Self-employment income is defined as net earnings from self-employment. This includes gross income derived from any trade or business (less any allowable deductions) and a partner's distributive share (whether distributed or not) of any partnership trade or business. Not considered self-employment income are the allocated earnings to shareholders from an S corporation.

Reimbursements received from clients must be included in income and are offset by claiming business expense deductions for amounts spent. ∎

The federal income tax structure is based on a pay-as-you-go system. Employees have certain amounts withheld from income during the year, with those amounts going directly to the IRS. If you're self-employed or you don't have enough tax withheld, you may pay estimated tax in installments up to four times a year. The rules governing the payment of such taxes and the penalties you can incur for underpayment are explained in this section.

Withholding of Taxes

If you're an employee, your employer will withhold tax from your income as you receive it during the year. Because of changes brought about by the passage of the Tax Reform Act of 1986, you'll need to be aware of how withholding works in order to avoid penalties for underpayment.

Withholding on employees' pay. Taxes will generally be withheld from the commissions, salaries and wages, bonuses, vacation and sick pay, taxable fringe benefits, and pensions and annuities of employees unless their income is so low that they're able to claim exemption from withholding. The amount withheld will depend on the amount of earnings and the information furnished on Form W-4—Employee's Withholding Allowance Certificate.

Form W-4. As a result of the great controversy over the complexity of the 1987 Form W-4, a simpler Form W-4A was later introduced. Basically, both forms require that you estimate in advance the amount of withholding that will be necessary to cover your final tax liability for the year. Complete only one Form W-4 unless you're married and you and your spouse are planning to file separate returns. For help in completing the form, ask for IRS Publication 505: *Tax Withholding and Estimated Tax.*

Information you give your employer on Form W-4 includes your marital status, the number of withholding allowances you're claiming, and any additional amounts you want withheld. The number of withholding allowances you can claim depends on the number of your exemptions and jobs, the amount of deductions and credits you expect to have, and, if married, any additional allowances claimed by your spouse on a separate W-4 (when you both work, you can divide the combined available allowances in any way you wish).

If you have substantial nonwage income or expect to claim tax credits on your return, you need to file the original Form W-4, since those additional withholding allowances are not provided for on Form W-4A. Any estimates used to figure additional withholding allowances can't be greater than the amount of that same item as reported on your previous year's return, plus any added amount related to an event that has happened or will happen during the current year.

If any information you gave on your W-4 or W-4A changes during the year, you need to file a new form within 10 days. To help you determine if you've completed the form correctly, call the IRS at 1-800-424-FORM (3676) and ask for Publication 919: *"Is My Withholding Correct?"*

Withholding on fringe benefits. Generally, your employer is required to withhold income tax on the fair market value of certain taxable noncash fringe benefits you receive, since they're considered part of compensation. The amount withheld can be 20% of their value or, as an alternative, their value can be added to your other pay, with the amount withheld based on the total.

Other types of withholding. Payments of sick pay made by your employer are subject to withholding. The same is true for payments distributed from a pension or annuity plan, unless you choose not to have tax withheld.

Withholding on commissions for nonemployees. Generally, compensation you receive if you're self-employed is not subject to withholding. However, under a concept called backup withholding, the payer must withhold 20% of the payments as income tax if any of the following applies:

1. They were required to give you a Form 1099 last year.
2. They made payments to you the previous year that were subject to backup withholding.

3. You fail to supply an identification number to the payer.

4. The payer is notified by the IRS that the number you furnished is incorrect.

5. You fail to certify that you're not subject to backup withholding when required to do so.

Severe penalties can be assessed for giving false or incomplete information in an attempt to avoid backup withholding.

Estimated Tax Payments

If you don't pay taxes through withholding or if the amounts withheld are not sufficient, you may have to pay estimated tax. This is the method used to pay income, self-employment, and any other taxes reported on Form 1040. In each year that you make estimated tax payments, you must file Form 1040, not 1040A or 1040EZ.

Who makes estimated payments? Under the new tax law, you should make estimated tax payments 1) if you think your estimated tax for the year will be $500 or more and 2) if you expect that your total income tax withheld for the year will be less than 90% of the current year's tax due *or* 100% of your last

year's tax (only if for a full year), whichever is less.

The amount owed is called your required annual payment and is usually made in four equal installments. Generally, you don't have to make those payments when all of your income is subject to withholding and you owe less than $500 when you file your return.

Married taxpayers can apply these rules on a joint basis (even if not living together) or on separate estimated income. But if you're separated under a decree of divorce or separate maintenance, you're not allowed to make joint estimated tax payments. The same is true if either you or your spouse is a nonresident alien or if you have different tax years. Whether you make estimated tax payments jointly or separately, you're still free to file either joint or separate tax returns.

Computing the tax. In order to figure how much tax you'll owe at the end of the year, you'll have to estimate your taxable income for the current year, a difficult task for outside salespeople whose income and expenses can fluctuate widely throughout the year. Use the worksheet that comes with Form 1040-ES, starting with your prior year's tax

21

return. Then consider any changes in your situation, as well as changes in the tax law. IRS Publication 505 can be of help if you're figuring your estimated tax yourself.

Estimated tax payments for the year include installment payments sent in with Form 1040-ES, any overpayment from last year that you want applied to this year's tax, income tax withheld from any source, and any credit for excess social security tax withheld. You're required to pay the installment amount on each due date in order to avoid penalties.

If you don't receive taxable income evenly throughout the year, you can use a formula called annualized income installment to determine the amount due for each payment period. Using this method, you may be able to pay less than the required annual payment for each due date and still avoid the underpayment penalty. Consult Publication 505.

When and how to pay. For calendar-year taxpayers, the specific payment due dates are the 15th of April, June, and September of the current year and January of the following year (different dates apply for fiscal-year taxpayers). If you don't receive any income on which you'll owe estimated tax until *after* a particular due date, simply spread the amount over the remaining due dates.

If amounts change after you've made your first estimated tax payment, you must refigure the total tax (use the *Amended Estimated Tax Schedule* in Form 1040-ES) and pay the balance over the remaining payment periods.

Self-employment Tax

The self-employment tax is nothing more than a social security tax for the self-employed. The tax provides retirement benefits and hospital insurance under Medicare. Generally, you estimate the tax for the year and pay it in installments. If you're in business for yourself, whether you're a sole proprietor, an independent contractor, or a partner, you're likely to owe self-employment tax.

The tax is paid on self-employment income (see page 18 for a definition). One spouse is not considered self-employed just because the other is; you each pay your own tax only on your own self-employment income. If one spouse merely provides services for the other spouse, the payments are not subject to either social security or self-employment tax.

Not considered self-employment income is compensation to you as an employee or officer of a corporation in which you own all or most of the stock. But any fee received for being a director is included in self-employment income.

To figure the tax, use Schedule SE, Form 1040. You'll need to determine the amount of your net earnings and the portion subject to the tax; then you multiply that amount by the tax rate. There are two methods to figure net earnings; both are explained in IRS Publication 505.

Claiming Your Payments & Withholding

When you file your tax return for the year, you simply compute the total amount of tax due and then subtract the amounts withheld together with the total of your estimated tax payments

Estimated tax and separate returns. If you and your spouse made separate estimated tax payments and file separate returns, you can only claim credit for your own payments. But if you made joint estimated tax payments, they can be divided between you in any of these ways:

1. One spouse claims all the tax and the other none.
2. You can agree to divide them any way you wish.
3. If you can't agree, you must divide the payments proportionately to the tax shown on each separate return.

The same choices are available if you were divorced during the year and you previously made joint estimated tax payments.

Withholding and separate returns. As with estimated tax, you can claim credit for tax withheld from your own income only if you're married and file separately. But in community property states, each spouse takes credit for half of all taxes withheld from community income. If you divorce during the year, you report half of the community income and the withholding on that income only for the part of the year before the divorce.

Excess social security (FICA) tax withheld. If you had too much social security tax withheld because you worked for more than one employer, you can claim the extra amount as a credit against any income tax you owe when you file your return.

Penalties for Underpayment

There are two ways in which you may have to pay penalties for underpaying taxes you owed. The first is when the net amount you owe when you file your Form 1040 is $500 or more and is also more than 10% of your total tax. The second is when any installment payment of estimated tax is less than the required amount for that particular due date, even if you're due a refund.

Form 2210—Underpayment of Estimated Tax by Individuals is used to compute any penalties that may be due. You can fill it out yourself or have your tax advisor do it. Otherwise, the IRS will do it for you and bill you. Even if you request a waiver of the penalty, you must still file the form.

Exceptions to paying penalties. In two situations, you don't have to file Form 2210 or pay any penalty at all. The first is when the total tax shown on page 2 of Form 1040 (less withholding, credits, and other payments) results in your owing less than $500.

The second is if you had no tax liability on your last year's return.

Waiver of penalty. The new tax law contains a special waiver provision if your underpayment (only for periods *before* April 16, 1987) was created or increased by any provision of the law itself.

The underpayment penalty can also be waived if payment wasn't made because of a casualty or an unusual occurrence, or if you retired or became disabled after reaching age 62 during the time a payment was due and you had reasonable cause for not making it. To claim a waiver of penalty, complete Part 1 of Form 2210, write "WAIVER" on the front, and attach an explanation. Be sure to show how much should be waived.

Period of underpayment. The penalty is computed for the number of days from the due date up to and including the date you paid or April 15, whichever is earlier. The penalty rate is currently 9%; since it changes often, call the IRS before you complete Form 2210. On page 2 of Form 1040, subtract any penalties you owe from any refund you have coming. ■

Reimbursements for expenses, with few exceptions, must be either deducted from total allowable expenses or included in income, whether the reimbursements are received from employers, clients, customers, or anyone else. Reimbursed or unreimbursed, and regardless of who eventually deducts them, deductible expenses must be ordinary and necessary to the operation of a trade or business.

Prior to 1987, all outside salespeople could deduct their business expenses whether or not they itemized their deductions. Under the Tax Reform Act of 1986, however, the preferential treatment for outside salespeople who are *employees* has been eliminated, as explained below. The rules have remained the same for the self-employed. Record reimbursements as you receive them on page 97.

Deductibility Rules for Employees

Employee expenses may be fully or partially reimbursed, or not reimbursed at all. In some cases,

reimbursements can even exceed expenses. The rules for each situation are explained below.

If you're an employee, you must now deduct unreimbursed expenses or expenses that exceed reimbursements as a miscellaneous deduction on Schedule A. Such expenses are deductible only to the extent that the total of your miscellaneous deductions exceeds 2% of your adjusted gross income. The 2% floor is applied to business-related meal and entertainment expenses after the 80% limitation discussed on page 57 is applied.

Tax$aver Tip. *Obtain a statement from your employer as to every type of expense that's reimbursable and try to avoid incurring any expenses that are not. If that's not possible, ask your employer to pay you a bonus equal to the 2% amount disallowed, provided you attain certain sales goals.*

Reporting on tax return not required. Suppose you properly account to your employer (by submitting a statement prepared from your daily records, along with receipts) and you're *fully reimbursed* for exactly the amount you spent. If the expenses were solely for the benefit of your employer, who then claims the deductions, you need *not* report any expenses or reimbursements. You do, however, have to keep records just as if *you* were claiming the expenses—you're simply reporting to your employer, not the IRS.

A few additional requirements for this non-reporting include the following:

1. You claim no added unreimbursed expenses on your return that relate to the same employer.
2. No personal expenses were reimbursed. (If they were, they must be considered as income.)
3. You and the employer are not related in any way.
4. You don't own more than 10% of the corporation's stock.

It's a good idea to attach a statement to your return that reimbursements from your employer did not exceed your deductible expenses.

If you use the standard mileage rate and your reimbursements are equal to the 22½¢ per mile rate, you're deemed to have made an accounting to your employer. You still must document the time, place, and business purpose of your expenses. There's no limitation on the number of miles you can drive under this arrangement.

Accounting to employer not required. Some employers simply pay a fixed amount each month for expenses. Those amounts are basically treated as additional wages and should be included as income on your W-2 form, since withholding of taxes is required. You can claim your reimbursed business expenses on Form 2106 as an offset to this income as long as you meet all required record-keeping rules. Without records, you'll end up paying tax on the reimbursements with *no* deductions.

Accounting to employer required. Many employers, as a matter of policy, require the reporting and documentation of actual expenses for reimbursement. Many also base auto expense reimbursements on the 22½¢ per mile rate and use established per diem rates to cover other expenses, such as meals, lodging, laundry, cleaning, and tips. Because per diem rates do not cover cab fares, telegrams, or telephone calls, you can deduct these.

Note that if you're away from home on a temporary assignment (see page 47), you can't use per diem rates to estimate allowable living expenses. You also can't use per diem rates if you own more than 10% of the company's stock. Instead, you must account for all your expenses in full.

Your actual expenses for a trip are treated as "accounted for" if the per diem you receive doesn't exceed the maximum established rate for the area. You don't have to get receipts for travel expenses, but you or your employer must still have records of the mileage, time, place, and business purpose of the travel.

Be sure to keep duplicates of all receipts and expense reports since your employer could have the expenses disallowed because of inadequate or lost substantiation. Without your copies, the reimbursements could be treated as income, and you'd be forced to pay the tax even though you had legitimate offsetting expenses and had supplied documentation.

When reimbursements exceed expenses. When your reimbursements exceed your expenses and are included on your W-2 form at the end of the year, you must file Form 2106 with your return to deduct your expenses, whether or not you account to your employer.

When your employer does *not* include reimbursements on your W-2 form and you're *not* required to account to your employer, you must also file Form 2106. Enter total reimbursements and expenses; then transfer the excess only to Form 1040.

If your employer requires an accounting but does not include reimbursements on your W-2, you don't have to file Form 2106. Simply include the excess amount of reimbursements over expenses on Form 1040. Otherwise, you'd be accounting to the IRS *and* to your employer.

If your employer chooses to reimburse you more than 22½¢ per mile for auto expenses, the *full* amount, not just the excess, must be reported on your W-2 form. You must then file Form 2106. You should then use the method which gives you the largest amount to figure your expenses, so that any taxable excess is reduced as much as possible. If you use the standard mileage rate, the entire excess will be taxable unless the IRS can be convinced that the excess payment was necessary, reasonable, and due to unusual circumstances.

When expenses exceed reimbursements. This situation is likely to occur when you use the actual cost method and your employer reimburses you at the 22½¢ per mile rate or reimburses you on a per diem basis. You're required by the IRS to file a detailed statement with your return, even if you used the standard mileage rate; the statement must include all advances, allowances and reimbursements received, expenses paid by you, and charges paid or borne by your employer. Also include in the statement evidence that will establish the elements of your expenses. This statement will help prevent an audit, but if it doesn't, you're likely to be asked to substantiate *all* your travel and entertainment expenses.

Use Form 2106 to report your excess expenses whether or not your reimbursements are included on your W-2 form. This excess is then transferred to and deducted on Schedule A.

Reimbursement available but not requested. Let's say your employer has a reimbursement plan but perhaps because of their cash flow problems, you didn't request reimbursement for employer expenses you've paid. In this case, *you lose your deduction forever*, since the IRS will not allow you to convert your employer's expenses into a deduction of your own simply because of your lack of action. When reimbursements are general policy but it's a condition of your employment not to receive any, deductions have, on rare occasions, been allowed. The moral: If you're entitled to reimbursement, request it, even if your employer doesn't pay it.

Unreimbursed expenses. Even if you're expected to pay certain expenses as a condition of your employment, deductibility is not assured. There should be a reasonable relationship between the expenditures and your compensation. Ask for a statement or corporate resolution which says your compensation is based on expecting you to incur various stated expenses. This will indicate to the IRS that it's *necessary* for you to pay such expenses and that the amount of your compensation has been taken into consideration to cover those expenses.

Keep in mind that with good records and whether reimbursed or not, you can deduct any business-related expenses that are necessary to do your job.

Other special situations. If you're related to your employer, all reimbursements, unless you're using the standard mileage rate, must be reported on your tax return as income. (Related means siblings, children, stepchildren, spouses, ancestors, and lineal descendants.)

Basically, the same rules apply if you and/or your relatives own more than 10% of the outstanding stock of the corporation which employs you. Unless you use the 22½¢ per mile rate, you must keep records for travel and entertainment expenses and report them on your return. This is also true if an unincorporated employer is a member of your family.

Any personal expenses—travel, meal, and lodging expenses for family members who accompany you on a business trip, for example—that are subsequently reimbursed to you must be included as income.

Reimbursements to the Self-employed

If you're self-employed and you incur expenses on behalf of your clients or customers and then you bill and collect those amounts, include the total in other income on Schedule C. Be sure to state meal and entertainment expenses separately; otherwise, you, not your client, will be subject to the 80% limitation rule.

In every instance, you must meet the substantiation requirements for travel, entertainment, or gift expenses that are reimbursed by your clients whether or not you account to them. Your clients are not required to substantiate reimbursements to you unless you properly account to them for such expenses.

Tax$aver Tip. *Always maintain your own records to substantiate each element of an expense; otherwise, you risk a double disallowance—to your client and to yourself.* ■

Deductible Expenses

For people in outside sales, automobile expenses are usually a major expense item, whether you or your employer pays for them. This section explains which auto expenses are deductible and how to compute your deduction.

For complete information about auto deductions, plus all the forms you'll need for a year's worth of record keeping, see *Sunset's Automobile Tax$aver.*

Local Transportation Expenses

Local transportation expenses are those incurred in order to get from point A to point B anywhere in the immediate geographical area of your work or business, generally referred to as your tax home (see page 143). This includes any trips during the work day *after* you arrive at work and *before* you depart for home, whether you're seeing customers or performing other business tasks.

Those local costs can be deducted, as long as they're ordinary and necessary, and related to the active conduct of your trade or business. Though those expenses typically relate to the operation and maintenance of your car (owned or leased), they can also include other forms of transportation, such as rail, bus, taxi, boat, or even airplane (commercial or private).

Local transportation does *not* include commuting—driving to your work site and returning home (see page 32).

Special rules for employees. According to the IRS, the general rule is that employees can treat local transportation as a business expense as long as it relates to their job. However, if the employee wishes to claim any depreciation, other requirements must be satisfied (see page 41).

Claiming expenses. Beginning in 1987, outside salespeople who are employees report local transportation expenses on Form 2106. Any excess of expenses over reimbursements is transferred to the miscellaneous deductions section of

Schedule A, Form 1040; only the miscellaneous deductions which exceed 2% of your adjusted gross income are deductible.

Self-employed outside salespeople use Schedule C and report local transportation expenses either separately or with other car expenses.

Commuting Expenses

Since the IRS has indefinitely suspended issuing any rulings on this subject, information and direction are being provided mainly by the courts. They say simply that "commuting is commuting, regardless of the nature of the work engaged in, the distance traveled or the mode of transportation used." (If you commute in a company-provided vehicle, see page 36 for information about valuation rules.)

The basic principle is that travel (in the general area of your tax home) from your residence to your *first* job location and from your *last* job location to your home is not a deductible expense, even when your first and/or last stop is your principal place of business or a client or customer's place of business.

Exceptions to basic commuting rules. If your work assignment is minor or temporary, the daily transportation costs of travel between the area you normally work in and a location outside of this area are deductible. "Temporary" means the assignment must end within a fixed and reasonably short period of time; if it's definite from the beginning, it's considered a nondeductible commuting expense. If, after being temporary, the time period becomes definite, deductibility ceases at that time.

Expenses for permanent or indefinite assignments are not deductible, even when the location is remote and no public transportation is available.

When a business trip by car requires that you be away from home one night, your travel costs are totally deductible and are *not* considered commuting. How far away from home must you travel? The Supreme Court has said simply that it's when you can't reasonably expect to leave from and return home at the start and finish of a day's work. And you needn't be gone for an entire 24-hour period or only during dusk-to-dawn hours. The time period you're away should be such that you'd need to get sleep or rest.

Eliminating or reducing commuting. An excellent way to eliminate commuting restrictions is to use your home as your regular place of work. This little-known tax break allows you to deduct all your local transportation costs as long as you satisfy all the rules for deducting a home office. Your first and last stops are now deductible, as well as all business travel in between.

If you're not able to meet the home office rules, it's wise tax planning to live as close as possible to your regular place of business so you can minimize your nondeductible commuting expense.

Examples of nondeductible commuting. The courts have declared the following situations to be nondeductible:

- Business discussions with business associates while driving to work
- Doing *any* kind of work in your car while driving to work, such as business calls
- Cost of commuting in a company car
- Driving a car that displays advertising
- Driving to any regular place of employment, regardless of the distance traveled
- Travel between a temporary residence and a regular place of employment

Tax$aver Tips. *Here are a few ideas that can save you tax dollars if they apply to you:*

- *Unless inconvenient, do any driving required by your job after the first stop or before the last stop of the day. Try to make your first and last stops as close to home as possible.*
- *When it's not reasonable or convenient to stop at the office before or after a long one-day trip outside your work area, you can deduct the cost of traveling from your home to the business location and back.*
- *If you have two cars, you may achieve some tax benefits, depending on the cost of the cars, by designating the more expensive one as your business car and the other as your personal car. On days when you're reasonably sure to be driving a lot of business miles, use the business car. When you think you'll drive very little for business during the day, drive the personal car. This will also help you maximize the business use percentage of the business car.*

33

Using a Company Car

If you're an employee or officer of a corporation, whether or not you're a stockholder (majority or minority), and you drive a company car, then it's especially important that you maintain complete records of auto use. Failure to do so can result in disastrous effects for both you and the company.

If the IRS audits the company and finds unsubstantiated expenses for which you have been reimbursed, the corporate deductions may be disallowed and additional tax may be due. And since you were reimbursed for a nondeductible expense, the payments are then classified as income to you, either as a dividend or extra compensation, and you may owe additional personal income tax. Thus, both you *and* the company may end up paying additional tax, plus interest, on the *same* disallowed expenses.

Many companies have included a clause in their bylaws stating that any stockholder must reimburse the corporation for any expenses disallowed by the IRS. This not only provides cash to the corporation but also allows the stockholder to deduct the reimbursement.

Accounting for personal use. When you keep an accurate record of your mileage, business and personal, and a fair market value (FMV) of the personal-use portion is determined under IRS rules, the corporation may treat the personal-use amount as additional compensation to you reported on Form W-2; as a dividend to you, in which case the corporation does not deduct the value of the personal use; or as part compensation, part dividend.

Documenting your expenses. Adequate records and substantiation will eliminate disallowances due solely to poor record keeping. As for the problem of personal use, it depends on how the IRS evaluates the facts and circumstances of each case.

To protect both you and the corporation, you can include in the corporate minutes a statement similar to this one:

Sue Curtis has been provided with a (*description of auto and FMV*) which is necessary for her duties as (*title or job description*), is for the convenience of the corporation, and is a condition of employment. It is recognized that there will be some personal use of this vehicle and that Ms. Curtis will supply the company with a mileage record of personal use. This mileage will be valued according to IRS rules, and the value so determined will be additional compensation and reported annually on her W-2 form. Ms. Curtis has also agreed to the withholding of all required taxes on this additional compensation.

Make sure the statement is dated and signed by the corporation and the employee and/or stockholder. Of course, the title to the car must be in the corporation's name.

An alternative method is for the corporation to charge the employee and/or stockholder for the value of the personal use. You write a check (nondeductible) payable to the corporation, which then credits it against the operating expenses of the car. The net result is that the corporation is only deducting the business-related portion of the car's cost, which is exactly what the IRS wants.

Tax$aver Tip. *Perhaps the most logical plan is for you to buy the company-owned car you're now using at the existing FMV or at the undepreciated amount on the company's books, whichever you and the company agree on. Then ask the company to set up a reimbursement plan, using either the standard mileage rate or the actual cost method, again whichever is most advantageous for the corporation and yourself.*

Use of an Auto as a Fringe Benefit

For many years, fringe benefits in general have been the single most volatile area of tax law. Since the rules change continually, we will offer only a cursory look at the subject as it pertains to automobiles. Generally, the current temporary regulations are effective retroactively to January 1, 1985.

Taxable fringe benefits. When your employer provides you with a car, the FMV of its personal use is included in your gross income, unless specifically excluded from income by other tax law or unless you've paid the company for the value of your personal use. The regulations provide both general and special rules that can be used to determine FMV.

The employee can use either the general or the special rules to value the benefit. If a special rule is used, it must be the same as that used by the employer. (This situation occurs when you use an employer-provided vehicle for both business and personal use and your employer included the full value of the car on your W-2 form.) You can then offset the income by claiming all your expenses on Form 2106. However, under the provisions of the Tax Reform Act of 1986, this adverse situation will always result in additional taxable income—you're reporting *all* the income, but you can only deduct expenses exceeding 2% of your adjusted gross income as a miscellaneous deduction on Schedule A.

Unless personal use of an employer-provided car is very minimal, you must report this use as a taxable fringe benefit (assuming the full value is not included on your W-2). Since the rules are complex, see your tax advisor.

Provision of fuel-in-kind may be valued at 5.5¢ per mile according to the regulations. Vehicles provided by employers for commuting have special optional valuation rules. This value is fixed at $1.50 for each one-way commute and applies to each person commuting in the vehicle. The employer must require that one or more employees commute in the car and have a written policy that it not be used for any but minimal personal purposes other than commuting. This rule does not apply to control employees (directors, officers, or anyone owning 1% or more of the company).

Nontaxable fringe benefits. Automobile benefits you receive are excluded from income if they qualify as a working condition or de minimis fringe benefit. A *working condition fringe* is what would be deductible by you as an ordinary and necessary business expense had you paid for it yourself, such as the use of a company car or the value of free or reduced-cost parking on or near your employer's premises.

A *de minimis fringe* is a benefit that is so minimal that accounting for it would not only be unreasonable but also administratively impractical. Occasional, infrequent personal use of a company car is considered a de minimis fringe.

Substantiation requirements. Whether you're including use of a car in income and deducting the expenses, or merely excluding fringe benefits from income, you must substantiate business and personal use of the car with sufficient evidence, just as you would to prove trade or business deductions.

If the issue of fringe benefits affects you in a major way, consult your tax advisor. For more detailed information, obtain Publication 525: *Taxable and Nontaxable Income* from your local IRS office.

Computing Your Deduction

You can use either of two authorized methods to determine your auto expenses. The simplest one, the standard mileage rate (SMR), is based on a fixed mileage rate established by the IRS. The other, the actual cost method (ACM), requires you to itemize each expense. A form that lets you compute your deduction under both methods is on page 121.

The standard mileage rate. SMR is the easiest way to figure your deduction, since it reduces record keeping to an absolute minimum.

You simply keep track of actual business miles driven during the year, whether locally or away from home, and multiply the total by the rate allowed, currently 22½¢ for the first 15,000 business miles and 11¢ per mile thereafter. Those rates are intended to cover most operating and fixed costs, including gas and oil, repairs and maintenance, supplies, licenses, insurance, and depreciation. Always add business parking fees and tolls and the business portion of property taxes to the computed deduction. If you're self-employed, you can also add the business portion of interest.

Because the deduction per business mile is fixed by the IRS, your total deduction simply depends on how many miles you drive. However, you still must record the dates of each use and the business or investment purpose (use the logs on pages 84 and 89).

Note that you can't use SMR if you lease the car, use it for hire, have claimed accelerated or additional first-year depreciation in a prior year, or use more than one car at the same time in the same business. If you don't qualify for SMR for any of these reasons, you'll have to use ACM.

The actual cost method. For ACM, you must keep a record of all the actual operating and fixed costs of your car, such as gas and oil, repairs and maintenance, supplies, interest, insurance, taxes, and, most importantly, depreciation.

If a car is used *exclusively* for business purposes, you can deduct all the costs of operation, except for interest if you're an employee. Typically, however, the car is used for both business and personal purposes, so an allocation of expenses must be made. Only the ordinary and necessary expenses directly attributable to business are deductible.

Computing your auto deduction under ACM is a four-step procedure:

1. Determine the percentage of business use of your car, usually by dividing total business miles for the year by total miles driven, to see if you meet the 50% test (see page 41).
2. Determine your total expenses for the year, exclusive of business parking fees and tolls.
3. Compute a new business use percentage, including any investment miles.
4. Multiply your total expenses by that business use percentage, and then add parking fees and tolls to determine your deduction for the year.

Claiming deductions. Under the Tax Reform Act of 1986, *employees* in outside sales report their business auto expenses on Form 2106 and deduct expenses in excess of reimbursements only as a miscellaneous deduction on Schedule A. All miscellaneous deductions are now subject to the 2% of adjusted gross income limitation.

Maintaining good records is essential, as employees will need to answer the following questions on Form 2106:

- Do you or your spouse have another vehicle available for personal purposes?
- If your employer provided you with a vehicle, is personal use during off duty hours permitted?
- Do you have evidence to support your deduction? If yes, is the evidence written?

You'll also have to report your average daily round-trip commuting distance and the total miles your car was used for commuting.

Self-employed persons claim auto deductions on Schedule C and are not subject to the 2% floor. They must also file Form 4562—Depreciation and Amortization, and answer similar questions about their auto use.

Though ACM involves more record keeping, it will usually result in greater tax savings, especially if you drive an expensive car. To save you some time, the IRS has approved a *sampling* method for taxpayers whose auto use is regular. The logic is this: if you maintain adequate, detailed records for only *part* of a tax year and can prove by other evidence that the period you chose is *typical* of your annual auto use, the business use percentage so established can be used without your having to keep records throughout the year.

Though you can choose your own sampling period, the IRS has made two suggestions:

1. Keep records for the first 3 months, determine your percentage, and use it for the year.
2. Maintain adequate records during the first week of every month.

Though the business use percentage in the second example won't be the same each month, it's assumed, though not yet clarified by the IRS, you'd simply average them and use that percentage for the entire year.

If you're using the sampling method, be sure you can prove that the periods chosen are repre-sentative of the rest of the year. Don't use it if your auto travel for business is unpredictable from day to day or week to week. Also, you can't use any sampling method if you drive your employer's car and it's available for use by any other employee for all or even part of the year. ∎

Depreciation

Depreciation is the process of deducting the cost or other basis of business or income-producing property over the estimated useful life of the asset. No deduction is allowed for personal use of business assets. To be depreciated, property must have a useful life of more than a year.

Your depreciation deduction for such items as your car, home computer, and home office is limited by your business use percentage (BUP). For help in determining your BUP, see pages 38, 64, and 76. Other property used exclusively for business can be depreciated in full and is not subject to allocation. If you place more than 40% of the property in service during the last 3 months of the year, special rules may apply for computing the deduction. See your tax advisor for details.

The Section 179 election allows you to deduct up to $10,000 ($5,000 before 1987) of the purchase price of depreciable business property the first year it's placed in service, as opposed to depreciating it over its useful life. The deduction is limited to the taxable income from the trade or business in which the property is used. Any amount so deducted reduces the basis. The $10,000 limit applies regardless of the number of assets placed in service that year.

Tax$aver Tip. *If you're reasonably sure you can meet the 50% test each year, elect Section 179 and deduct the maximum amount allowed (subject to BUP) the year the asset is placed in service.*

Any investment tax credit (ITC) claimed prior to its repeal date of January 1, 1986, is still subject to the recapture rules; also, the value of any remaining carryovers from prior years is reduced by 17½% for 1987 and by 35% thereafter.

Keep track of basis and depreciation on the form on page 82.

Depreciation of your home. The depreciation method you use depends on when you purchased your home and/or converted it to business use. If both occurred before 1980, you're subject to rules in effect at that time.

For property purchased or placed in service between 1981 and December 31, 1986, you're required to use the accelerated cost recovery system (ACRS), choosing either the accelerated method with fixed percentages each year or an alternate method with percentages based on straight-line (pro-rata) depreciation. Regardless of the method, you compute your deduction by multiplying the fixed percentage for the year by the unadjusted basis (after subtracting the estimated value of the land).

The Tax Reform Act of 1986 (TRA '86) has changed ACRS. Residential property (which is not rented but is used in your business) purchased and/or placed in service on or after January 1, 1987, can now only be depreciated over 27½ years using the straight-line method.

Listed property rules. The IRS has established listed property rules designed to curb deductions and credits for certain types of assets commonly used for both business and personal purposes. Included under these rules are home computers, cars, light trucks not used for hire, airplanes, and boats.

Any listed property placed in service after June 18, 1984, must be used more than 50% in a qualified trade or business (exclusive of any investment use) each year of its useful life, or it's subject to special rules. If the 50% test is not met in the *first* year of service, the following limitations apply:

1. No Section 179 expense can be claimed.
2. No accelerated depreciation is allowed.
3. Depreciation must be computed under the straight-line method and different lives may apply.

When you meet the 50% test the first year but in any later year your business use percentage falls to 50% or less, you must recapture at least a portion of any investment tax credit previously claimed, as well as all Section 179 expense and all accelerated depreciation claimed in excess of what would have been claimed under the straight-line method.

Depreciating your car. The combined depreciation and Section 179 deduction has been further limited by the new tax law. For a car placed in service

41

after December 31, 1986, only $2,560 is allowed the first year, $4,100 the second year, $2,450 the third year, and $1,475 each year thereafter.

Cars are now 5-year property. If you meet the 50% test and buy a car after December 31, 1986, you can depreciate it over 5 years, using the 200% declining balance method, with a switch to straight line when it yields a larger deduction. Or you can elect to depreciate the car over 5 years using the straight-line method. If you fail to meet the 50% test, the car is still 5-year property, but you *must* use straight line and your deduction can't exceed what it would have been under the accelerated method.

Regardless of the date the car was placed in service, the amount must be further reduced by applying your BUP. Since a car is listed property, the rules discussed on page 41 apply.

Depreciating a home computer. A computer placed in service after December 31, 1986, and used more than 50% for trade or business is 5-year property and is depreciated using the 200% declining balance method (in lieu of prescribed percentages), with a switch to straight line when it yields a larger deduction. Or you can elect to

depreciate the computer over 5 years using the straight-line method. If you don't meet the 50% test, you *must* depreciate it over 5 years under straight line. Whether or not you meet the test, you need to reduce the amount by applying your BUP.

If you meet the 50% test, you can increase your depreciation deduction by including any use connected with investment activities in your BUP.

Unless your computer is used *exclusively* at a regular business establishment, which can include a home office, it's subject to the listed property rules discussed on page 41.

Office furniture and equipment. Items used exclusively for business purposes must be depreciated if they have a useful life longer than a year. They must be assets that wear out, become obsolete, or simply decline in value over time. Most of these, if purchased before 1987, are probably in the 5-year class under ACRS (12 years under the alternate straight-line method). However, under the new tax law, assets of this type placed in service after December 31, 1986, must now be depreciated over 7 years under either the 200% declining balance method or the straight-line method.

Improvements to your property. Often, there's a gray area between what constitutes an improvement, which must be depreciated, and what constitutes a repair (see below), which is deductible in the year paid.

The IRS says you must depreciate the cost of an improvement if it increases the value of the improved property, lengthens its life, or makes it more useful. Similarly, replacements that stop deterioration and add to an asset's life must also be depreciated.

If the improvement benefits only the business part of your home office, you can depreciate the entire cost. But if it benefits your entire home, you can only depreciate based on your BUP.

Repairs to your home or office. An expenditure for a repair, as opposed to an improvement, is deductible in the year paid. Repairs may also have to be allocated according to business use. A furnace repair, for example, benefits your entire home; if 15% of your home is used as an office, you can deduct 15% of the repair bill, including parts, supplies, and labor (but not your own).

Repairs are what keep something in normal working order over its useful life; they're usually not of a major nature. (This doesn't mean the repair can't be expensive.) Repairs should not prolong the property's life, make it more useful, add to its value, or be part of a general plan of improvement. ■

Leasing Business Assets

Often, leasing business assets can be more advantageous than purchasing them outright, since only a minimum outlay of cash is necessary when you lease. But just because an agreement is called a lease doesn't automatically convince the IRS that it's not a conditional sales contract. If it's found to be a sales contract, all lease payments are applied to the purchase price, and interest and depreciation will be calculated just as if you owned the property.

The IRS has issued seven conditions which indicate that a lease should be treated as a conditional sale for tax purposes. If any one of these apply to your agreement, you just made a purchase.

1. The agreement applies part of each "rent" payment toward an equity interest you'll receive.
2. You get title to the property after making all the required payments.
3. You must pay an amount close to the cost of the property over a time period that's shorter than the expected useful life of the property, and you may continue to use it for nominal payments for an additional amount of time approximating its remaining estimated useful life.
4. You pay rent that is much more than the property's current fair rental value.
5. You have an option to buy the property at a price that is low compared to its value at the time you may take advantage of the option. (You should determine this value at the time of the agreement.)
6. You have an option to buy the property at a price that is low compared to the total amount you are required to pay under the lease.
7. The lease designates some part of the "rent" payments as interest, or part of the "rent" payments are easy to recognize as interest.

If your intent is to enter into a true lease, make sure *none* of the above appears in your agreement. However, if, under a lease agreement, you placed property in service between January 1, 1981, and December 31, 1983, your transaction is guaranteed by the IRS to be treated as a lease for tax purposes if certain requirements are met.

Terminal rental adjustment clause (TRAC). This is a clause in a motor vehicle agreement that requires or allows the lessor to adjust the final payment on the lease based on the difference between a projection of the car's value when the lease is signed and its actual value at the time of the final payment. The rules differ depending on whether the lease agreement is dated before or after October 16, 1984. Consult your tax advisor if this situation applies to you.

Types of leases. True leases, where you simply rent property for a specific period of time, are called operating leases and are not conditional sales contracts. They're typically either open- or closed-end leases.

An open-end lease can either make or cost you money when the lease expires. When you sign the lease, a specified resale value is agreed to. If the property sells for more, you get the excess; if it sells for less, you owe the difference. This type of lease is usually lowest in cost.

A closed-end lease (usually more costly) allows you to turn in the property with *no liability* for its resale price. But there are some closed-end leases that protect you against any resale loss, yet allow you to share in resale gains.

Tax effects of leasing. It's simply not true that leasing gives you tax breaks not available to owners. The expenses of operating business assets are always deductible, whether you own or lease. Trying to create quicker write-offs through lease payments will usually be ineffective, due to the availability of accelerated depreciation for owners. And because the IRS requires any advance lease payments to be deducted over the term of the lease, paying in advance doesn't work either. Of course, there are cases where deductible lease payments are higher than monthly depreciation expense.

If you leased a luxury car or home computer used in business after June 18, 1984, certain rules may limit the amount of your deductible lease payments and subject you to recapture of any investment tax credit previously claimed (see page 41). In the long run, you may find that lease costs yield substantially the same tax benefits as depreciation and interest on property you own. ■

Away-from-Home Expenses

Travel expenses while you're away from home overnight are deductible if they're directly related to the active conduct of your trade or business. They must be ordinary, necessary, and reasonable in amount and can never be for personal or vacation reasons.

Included as travel expenses are the costs of getting to and from a business destination, meals and lodging en route and while there, and other incidental expenses. Travel expenses can be deducted, within certain limitations, by both employees and the self-employed, whether or not those expenses are reimbursed.

Forms for recording away-from-home expenses begin on page 110.

What does "away from home" mean? The IRS has ruled that your tax home, for purposes of deducting travel expenses, is considered to be in one of two places. The first, which applies to most outside salespeople, is your regular *or* principal (if you have more than one regular) place of business.

The second is your regular place of abode in a real and substantial sense if, because of the nature of your business, you have no regular or principal place of business. The term tax home doesn't mean a particular building, but rather the entire city or general area where the taxpayer's business or work is located.

If you regularly work in two or more areas or businesses, use the following factors to help determine your main place of business:

1. The amount of time you ordinarily spend working in each area
2. The degree of activity in each business area
3. The income you earn in each area

The IRS and the courts are not in agreement about whether time spent or money earned is the principal test; however, for employees, income is the more significant factor.

Sleep and rest rule. In order for business meals and lodging to be deductible, you must be away from home on business overnight. "Overnight" means longer than an ordinary day's work, when you could not reasonably be expected to return without getting some sleep or rest, which does not include napping in your car. You don't have to be away from dusk until dawn or even for an entire day as long as the sleep or rest is necessary.

Temporary assignment or indefinite employment.

Travel expenses while away from home for temporary employment are deductible; those incurred as a result of indefinite employment are not. It's important that this determination be made *before* you begin work. Thus, you should think, intend, or have reason to believe the position is temporary for the away-from-home expenses to be deductible.

Temporary assignments are those whose termination can be foreseen within a fixed and reasonably short period of time. During this time, your tax home doesn't change. Generally, an assignment is considered temporary if it lasts less than a year. A stay of more than a year but less than 2 years may be considered temporary if certain conditions are met (see your tax advisor).

The advantage of temporary status is that you can deduct meal and lodging expenses even on your days off, since you're considered to be away from home. You can also deduct the commuting expenses between your residence (tax home) and your temporary job location; therefore, if you return home on weekends, you can deduct your travel, meal, and lodging expenses to and from your home. However, your deductions cannot exceed the meal and lodging expenses you would have incurred had you stayed at the temporary job location. If you kept a hotel room while you were away, you can deduct *only* the amount you would have spent for meals had you stayed.

Deductible without limitation are the first and final trips to the temporary job location. You can even deduct the daily commute costs to your tax home, but not if the temporary assignment is in your tax home area.

Indefinite assignments are those whose end can't be predicted within a fixed and reasonably short time. Generally, an assignment is considered indefinite if it lasts 2 years or more, regardless of other circumstances. The new location becomes your tax home, and you can't deduct travel to and from your home, transportation within the area, or meals and lodging while there.

If you're required to move for a probationary period, the assignment is considered indefinite and no deductions are allowed for meals and lodging. Assignments originally thought to be for more than 2 years but which are shortened for some reason can't be switched to temporary status—the determination must be made at the beginning. Any allowances you receive for travel or living expenses must be included in your income.

If all other rules and tests are met, you can deduct moving expenses, however.

Deductible travel expenses. Only certain expenses are deductible as travel expenses. Under the Tax Reform Act of 1986 (TRA '86), meals away from home, formerly reported as a travel expense, must now be reported separately. This is because under the new law, only 80% of the cost of such meals and entertainment is deductible. Included in the total amount subject to the limitation are taxes and tips, but not transportation costs to and from a business meal. If you're reimbursed for business meals, the 80% limitation applies to your employer, not to you. In addition, business meals must meet the same tests as business entertainment (see page 54).

If your meals away from home are reimbursed and their cost is relatively low, you can use a standard meal allowance of $14 per day for trips of less than 30 days ($9 if they're for 30 days or more) and avoid some record keeping. You still must establish the costs of other expenses plus the time, place, and business purpose of your travel. If you choose the optional method, it must be used for the entire tax year—you can't switch back and forth.

Tax$aver Tip. *Since you don't need receipts for expenditures under $25 (except for lodging), you'll get a larger deduction by simply entering the actual amounts in your records as they occur, rather than using the standard meal allowance.*

The use of a private plane is a perfectly acceptable mode of transportation for business travel, especially for outside salespeople who can cover their sales territory more effectively that way. The same listed property rules apply to private aircraft as they do to automobiles and computers (see page 41).

Luxury water travel. Under the new tax law, deductions for transportation by ocean liner, cruise ship, or other means of water transport are limited to twice the highest daily amount for per diem travel allowable to federal employees who are away from home but within the U.S. Check with your tax advisor or the IRS for the highest current rate. This limitation does not apply to expenses allowable for a convention, seminar, or other meeting held on a cruise ship (see page 53). Daily expenses for meals and entertainment are included in this per diem limitation, but must first be reduced by 20%.

Combined Business & Pleasure Travel

In an audit, the IRS will look closely at any business trip that might have combined business and pleasure.

Trips entirely for *business* reasons are fully deductible as long as the expenses incurred are ordinary and necessary. Conversely, trips entirely for *personal* purposes offer no deductions at all.

The gray area is when business and pleasure are combined. In this case, the IRS will try to determine the primary purpose of the trip; whether or not the IRS allows the deductions depends on the facts and circumstances of each case. Deductions are allowed whether you're an employee or self-employed.

What does "primary" mean? The most important consideration, according to the courts, is the *actual time* spent on business compared with that spent on personal or pleasure activities. (Use a diary to keep track of the hours spent on both.) Another consideration is the business destination's desirability as a resort area—the more preferred your destination is as a vacation site, the more important your documentation becomes.

Primary purpose is business. Let's say you travel to San Francisco on business, but you also extend your stay for a short vacation. Though you can't deduct any vacation expenses, you or your company can still deduct the travel expenses to and from San Francisco, as well as other business expenses. In other words, deduct only the business

49

expenses, just as if the trip were for business only. If you document the pleasure part of the trip, too, you'll have even better evidence if you're audited.

Primary purpose is pleasure. Travel expenses for a trip whose primary purpose is pleasure are *not* deductible, even if you engage in minor business activity. However, once you get to your destination (even at a side-trip location), you can always deduct expenses which are directly and properly for business reasons, just as if you were doing business at home.

Travel expenses of spouse and family. When a spouse or other family member accompanies you on a business trip or to a business convention, it must be adequately shown that the person's presence on the trip has a distinct business, rather than social, purpose in order to deduct their travel expenses. Performing incidental services or helping entertain business associates is not considered an acceptable business purpose.

When reimbursements for your spouse's expenses are received from your employer, the rules are the same as for you. The amounts are included in your income unless it's clearly established to be an ordinary and necessary business expense, and unless the person's presence was of substantial benefit, not merely helpful, to the conduct of business. Unless these conditions are proven, the costs of a family member's travel, meals, and lodging are *not* deductible.

Tax$aver Tips. *To help establish business purpose, consider obtaining a corporate resolution or statement detailing exactly what the person is to accomplish. Then keep a diary of those activities, describing in detail the activity the person was engaged in: what services, if any, were contributed and what meetings or social events were attended. Record the hours spent on each activity and show whether attendance was required or voluntary. Also note the business reason or benefit expected or received.*

*One factor the courts will consider is whether or not the person assists in **nontraveling** business activities during the* *year. If so, it's wise to maintain a diary of those activities, also.*

If your spouse travels with you but you're not deducting spousal expenses, don't limit your lodging deductions to only half the double-room rate. The IRS has said you can deduct the full cost of a single room, which usually results in a larger deduction. (Be sure to get proof of the single-room rate.) The same rule applies to special two-party airfares.

Travel outside the U.S. The rules for foreign travel are the same as for travel within the U.S. as long as the trip is *entirely* for business with no expenses subject to allocation. Similarly, no allocation is required for trips *primarily* for business if you meet at least one of the following conditions:

1. You were outside the U.S. for a week or less, regardless of the number of business or personal days. For the week, count the day you returned but not the day you left.
2. You spent *less* than 25% of the time for personal reasons and you were away more than a week. Count the day you left and the day you returned as business days.
3. You had no substantial control (not just the timing) about arranging the trip. (You're generally thought to have substantial control if you're self-employed.)
4. You're an employee unrelated to your employer, you're not a managing executive (who can decide on a trip without being vetoed), nor have you received a reimbursement or travel allowance.
5. You establish that a personal vacation was not a major consideration in making the trip, even if you had substantial control, own your business, are related to your employer, or are a managing executive.

If you don't meet any of the above conditions, you must allocate your expenses (round-trip transportation and meals and lodging en route) on the basis of time spent (days or hours) on business and personal matters.

Tax$aver Tip. *Though using days is easier, in certain cases hours could result in a larger* *deduction. Use the latter method when the amount of personal activities is small, since you can count sleep hours as business time on business days.*

"Business days" include the following:

1. Each day you're en route to or from a business destination by a reasonably direct uninterrupted route
2. Days you conduct your business during normal working hours
3. Days you're required to be somewhere for specific business reasons
4. Any day you're unable to work for reasons beyond your control
5. Weekends, holidays, and other necessary standby days if they fall between business days

Personal days are travel days for nonbusiness side trips, nonbusiness activities at the business destination (if a full day), and any days spent after all business has been concluded.

If you stop for a vacation while en route to or from your business destination, you must allocate expenses based on the cost from the U.S. to the

vacation site. The trip to or from the vacation site to the business location is considered as being entirely for business.

Conventions & Seminars

You can deduct travel expenses to attend a convention, seminar, or similar meeting if you can prove that the benefits were to you and were clearly related to your business duties. The cost of personal activities is not deductible, nor are costs associated with political conventions or meetings.

The IRS is particularly suspicious when a convention, trip, or cruise is sponsored by a trade organization and appears to be a disguised vacation. If abuse is suspected, the IRS may request the names and addresses of all participants. The courts place the greatest emphasis on the amount of time devoted to business compared with other activities; they also consider whether you were compelled to attend by your employer and where the meeting was held. (Deductions can't be disallowed solely because of the location.)

Beginning in 1987, deductions for travel, meal, and entertainment expenses associated with convention-related activities where minimal business matters are discussed are disallowed, as are deductions for attending a convention or seminar for investment purposes, financial planning, or other income-producing activity.

Special foreign rules. Special rules apply to activities held outside the "North American Area," which includes the U.S. and its possessions, Canada, Mexico, the Trust Territory of the Pacific Islands, the Marshall Islands, and the Federated States of Micronesia.

A meeting held outside this area is deductible if it's directly related to the active conduct of business and if it's "as reasonable" to hold the meeting outside the North American Area as within it, taking the following factors into account:

1. The purpose of the meeting and activities
2. The purpose and activities of the sponsoring organization
3. The places of residence of the active members or sponsors and places where other meetings have been or will be held
4. Any other factors thought relevant by the taxpayer

For special provisions and conditions regarding conventions held in Jamaica and certain Caribbean Basin countries, see your tax advisor.

You can always deduct the expenses of attending a foreign convention as long as the amount is included on Form W-2 or Form 1099.

Cruise ships. You can deduct a maximum of $2,000 for conventions, seminars, and similar meetings held on a U.S. flag cruise ship as long as the meetings are directly related to the active conduct of business and all ports of call are within the U.S. or its possessions. You must attach two written statements about the cruise to your tax return—one signed by you and one by an officer of the sponsoring group. ■

Entertainment Expenses

When you're in sales, entertaining customers and prospective customers is a common practice. Because the term entertainment is broadly construed, covering any activity of a type generally considered to constitute entertainment, recreation, or amusement, there's a lot of potential for abuse. It's easy to understand, then, why the IRS is so suspicious of entertainment expenses claimed by taxpayers and why the rules have consistently become stricter and more specific.

Basic rules. As with other business expenses, entertainment costs are deductible only if they are ordinary and necessary (see page 142) to the operation of a business you regularly carry on. They must also pass either the directly related or the associated with test.

The *directly related* test can be satisfied only if all the following requirements are met:

1. You had *more* than a general expectation of producing income or any other benefit at some future date, other than goodwill (though income or benefit doesn't have to result from each event).
2. During the entertainment period, you actively engaged in a business meeting, discussion, negotiation, or transaction with the person(s) being entertained.
3. The principal purpose of the entertainment was business, though it's not essential that you devote the majority of time to business to satisfy this requirement.
4. The money spent was allocable to the person(s) with whom you engaged in the active conduct of business during the entertainment.

You can also satisfy the directly related test if the entertainment occurred in a clear business setting which directly furthered your business.

Entertainment expenses are also deductible when considered *associated with* the active conduct of your trade or business. You must establish a clear business purpose for the entertainment, and it must be either directly preceded or followed by a substantial business discussion. Whether a business discussion is substantial or not depends on the facts and circumstances of each case. Usually, this requirement will be satisfied if you verify that the principal character or aspect of the combined activity was the active conduct of business.

> **Tax$aver Tip.** *Though a business discussion or meeting will usually occur on the same day as the entertainment, it could take place a day apart, such as when someone arrives from out of town.*

Entertaining for goodwill is a legitimate objective of any business in order to create, foster, and keep business customers. Though there are restrictions on entertainment for purposes of generating goodwill, such expenses can't be disallowed for that reason alone. According to the IRS, goodwill expenses are deductible in the following cases:

1. In limited situations under the directly related rule where the entertainment occurs in a clear business setting
2. When associated with the active conduct of business and the entertainment directly precedes or follows a substantial or bona fide business discussion

To properly substantiate entertainment expenses, you must record and prove all the following required elements of the expense:

1. The amount of each separate entertainment expenditure, including tips (incidental items can be totaled daily)
2. The date, place, and type of entertainment, and when and how long business was discussed
3. The nature of the discussion, its business reason, or the business benefit gained or expected
4. The name, title, and occupation of each person entertained, and who discussed business

Who you can entertain. IRS regulations state that the people you can reasonably expect to engage or deal with in your trade or business include customers, suppliers, employees, agents, partners,

55

and professional advisors, whether established or prospective.

The expenses of your spouse are also deductible if it's impractical under the circumstances to entertain without your spouse. You can deduct costs related to other family members only if they assist in a business manner or provide a service.

Strictly speaking, your own meal is deductible only as to the amount that exceeds what you would have ordinarily spent. But this rule actually applies only to abusive cases where a taxpayer tries to deduct a substantial portion of personal living expenses. In practice, the IRS typically allows the full cost of all meals to be deducted.

Where you can entertain. You can entertain for business in a variety of places, including your home, an airplane or boat, a restaurant or club, a hotel suite, or even a hunting lodge. No matter how often you use a particular facility, you generally can't deduct any depreciation or operating expenses for that facility.

The only exception to the above rule is that you may be able to deduct the dues paid to a country, social, athletic, or sporting club. You must use the club primarily (more than 50% of the time) to further your business. Also, you can deduct only that portion of the dues which meets the directly related and associated with tests.

However, you can only apply the directly related percentage against your dues in determining your deduction. You can compute this percentage based on business use (in days or hours) compared to all uses, or on the actual dollars spent for directly related business purposes compared to all others. The time the facility is merely available for use is ignored. You can count a day as business use even if you used the club for personal reasons the same day.

One-time initiation or membership fees are a nondeductible capital expense if the membership's useful life is longer than a year. If you later dispose of the membership, you must treat it as a disposition of two pieces of property, claiming any gain on both the business and personal portion but deducting only the business portion of a loss.

What you can deduct. Basically, you can deduct all the *direct* costs of each entertainment event, including food, beverages (even when nothing else is served), catering, music, waiters, invitations, and cleanup. You can also host a testimonial dinner and deduct the cost as long as it's under $400. If you entertain for business on a boat or plane, you can deduct gas and oil expenses.

Deductions not allowed. The IRS and the courts have disallowed entertainment deductions for the following:

- Expenses that are lavish or extravagant, or that are estimates or approximations
- Expenses that an employee doesn't ask the employer to reimburse or that an employer refuses to reimburse
- Expenses for entertaining large groups at home
- Meals or entertainment when you and your business associates take turns frequently in paying for the expenses

Tax$aver Tips. *You must always show that entertainment expenses are for business, not social purposes. It's also important to show through contemporaneous records the close timing between entertainment and a business discussion. Otherwise, you must meet the directly related test.*

If you're an employee who is expected to incur entertainment expenses and your employer takes this into consideration in determining your compensation, get a statement to that effect.

New rules on deductibility. The Tax Reform Act of 1986 sets new limitations on business meal and entertainment deductions, including expenses incurred away from home. Your allowable deduction is reduced to 80% of the total expenditure, and, for meals, no deduction is allowed unless business was discussed either during or directly before or after the meal. However, if you're away from home on business and you eat alone or with persons who are not business-connected, the business discussion rule does not apply.

There's no deduction if neither you nor an employee of yours is present when the food is furnished. Independent contractors are considered employees for this purpose.

57

The 20% reduction rule does not apply to such events as employee outings or Christmas parties, nor to expenses treated as fully taxable compensation to you or excludable as tax-free de minimis fringe benefits. The costs of getting to and from a business meal or entertainment are not subject to the 20% reduction.

Except for entertainment tickets purchased for certain charitable fund-raising sports events, the cost of any tickets you purchase (such as season tickets for theater or for athletic teams) is limited to the face value of the tickets *before* applying the 80% rule.

The new law also restricts your deduction for skyboxes or other private luxury boxes leased for more than one event at a sports arena. The deduction can't exceed the face value of the highest priced nonluxury box seat tickets generally made available to the public. (A special phase-in rule allows you to deduct two-thirds of the excess cost in 1987 and one-third in 1988.) Not included in this limitation are separately stated charges for food, beverages, or other services, though such charges are still subject to the 80% rule.

Employees claim entertainment expenses only as a miscellaneous deduction on Schedule A if they itemize. Only the amount of all miscellaneous deductions that exceeds 2% of adjusted gross income is deductible. The self-employed still claim their entertainment expenses (subject to the new 80% rule) on Schedule C. ■

Like many outside salespeople, you may maintain an office in your home from where you conduct your business. In order to claim home office deductions, you must use your office exclusively and regularly in a profit-seeking business, and very specific tests must be met. The business, however, does not have to be your *principal* business; it can be any business in which you're engaged, even part-time.

The rules for the storage of inventory are also explained here. And if you have a home computer used for business, you may be entitled to deductions even if you don't satisfy the home office rules.

Beginning in 1987, the deduction for home office use can't exceed your *net*, not gross, income from the business (see page 78 for information on the income limitations). Though a 1985 court case decided that these limits do *not* apply when employees lease a portion of their home to their employers, the Tax Reform Act of 1986 bars such a deduction. This also applies to a self-employed salesperson who leases to someone for whom services are performed.

If you fail to meet the tests or your home doesn't qualify for storage of inventory, you'll be denied a deduction for direct and indirect expenses (see page 77). Remember, however, that you're losing only *those* deductions. You can still use your home for business and deduct, with no restrictions, any ordinary and necessary business expenses. However, under the new law, all unreimbursed expenses of employees are deductible only for the amount that exceeds 2% of adjusted gross income.

Since the rules relating to deductible home office expenses are complex and constantly changing, see *Sunset's Home Office Tax$aver* or your tax advisor for additional information.

Basic Rules

First of all, for purposes of home office rules, what is a home? The IRS says a dwelling unit can be an apartment, boat, condominium, house, mobile home, or other similar property. An unattached garage, studio, barn, greenhouse, or any other structure on the property that relates to use as living accommodations is also included in this definition.

Who deducts home office expenses? *Self-employed outside salespeople* whose only office space is in their home will most likely be able to satisfy all the requirements. If you're an *employee* in outside sales, however, even if every other test is met, no deductions will be allowed unless the office is maintained solely for the *convenience of your employer*, not your own convenience. It's not enough that the office be appropriate and helpful to your duties; it must be *required* by your employer and be reasonably related to the nature of your job. If your employer also supplies you with an office, you should be able to show why it's inadequate.

Interestingly, the IRS has not clearly defined the term convenience of employer, but instead considers the facts and circumstances of each case. This gives you some latitude as to how you and your employer interpret this quasi-rule. Keep

in mind that the courts have ruled that your employer's principal place of business is not necessarily *your* principal place of business.

Tax$aver Tip. *Tax advisors generally agree that employees should obtain a statement or resolution clearly stating that an office at home is convenient for the employer, not for the employee.*

The Use Tests

To claim a home office deduction, you must prove that your home office is used both exclusively and regularly for business purposes. In addition, you must also prove that it meets at least *one* of the following three tests:

1. It's your principal place of business.
2. It's a place to meet customers or clients.
3. It's a separate structure not attached to your home.

Exclusive use test. Though much has been written about this test, it simply means that whatever *space* in your home is specified as being used for your business can't be used for *any other purpose* by you or any members of your family during the taxable year. If you use it for *both* business and personal purposes, you don't meet the test and your deductions will automatically be disallowed.

Where your home office is located is very important, should you be audited. Dens used to be a major concern of the IRS; in one of their examples, they said that if the den was also used for personal purposes, you could not claim any deductions for business use. But the code does not use the word "room"; thus, the courts have overruled the IRS and said that the business space doesn't have to be entirely separate.

IRS regulations now state that "the phrase 'a portion of the dwelling unit' refers to a room or other separately identifiable space; it is not necessary that the portion be marked off by a permanent partition."

Whatever space is used must relate directly to your business, so be sure it doesn't contain any nonbusiness items. If you have a computer, move it elsewhere when you use it for personal reasons.

You do *not* have to meet the exclusive use test if you use your home for storing inventory.

Regular use test. Once you satisfy the difficult exclusive use test, you must also prove that you use the space on a regular, continuing basis, not just incidentally or occasionally. But the guidelines are vague, stating only that "the determination whether a taxpayer has used a portion of the dwelling unit for a particular purpose on a regular basis must be made in light of all the facts and circumstances." Your best protection is to keep a diary describing the hours and business purpose of each use.

Principal place of business test. This test, the first of the three specified tests mentioned earlier, says that the business space in your home must be used exclusively and regularly as the principal place of business for *any* business you operate. The word "any" is important here because Treasury regulations say that "a taxpayer is deemed to have a principal place of business for each trade or business in which the taxpayer engages."

If you're engaged in only one business but at

more than one location, you must determine which location is the principal one. To make this determination, the IRS takes into account the following:

1. The portion of total income from the business attributable to activities at each location
2. The amount of time spent in activities related to that business at each location
3. The facilities available to the taxpayer at each location for purposes of that business

Since most of an outside salesperson's income is likely to be earned in the field, the last two factors will be considerably more important in making this determination.

Other factors to weigh are the importance of the business functions performed in the home, the business necessity of maintaining an office, and the costs to establish it.

Place to meet with customers test. To meet this test, the business space in your home must be used exclusively and regularly as a place to meet with clients or customers. They must be physically present on the premises.

The rules also say that the use by clients or customers must be substantial and integral to the conduct of your business. You can meet this test, yet still conduct business primarily at a location other than your home.

Use of a separate structure not attached to your home. The last of the three tests is perhaps the easiest to meet. Examples of separate structures are a barn, cottage or guest house, detached garage, greenhouse, studio, and workshop. Any exclusive and regular business connection will satisfy this test, even if you only make telephone calls there.

Storage of Inventory

As with a home office, you're allowed to deduct certain ordinary and necessary expenses for any portion of your home that you use on a regular basis to store inventory and goods you sell at wholesale or retail in your business. Such use of your home exempts you from the exclusive use test described on page 60.

Tests you must meet. The IRS regulations state that "the storage unit includes only the space actually used for storage; thus, if a taxpayer stores inventory in one portion of a basement, the storage unit includes only that portion even if the taxpayer makes no use of the rest of the basement.'' You can still use the remaining area for personal purposes.

In order to deduct expenses, you must meet all of the following tests:

1. The inventory must be held for use in your business.
2. Your business must be the selling of a product at either wholesale or retail, which includes mail order.
3. Your home must be the sole fixed location of that business.
4. The space used must be a separately identifiable section of your home and be suitable for storage.
5. The space must be used on a regular basis. Incidental or occasional use, even if exclusive, will not suffice. The rules do say, however, that use on a regular basis will be determined in light of all the facts and circumstances.

What you can deduct. Any expenses, such as repairs or maintenance, that relate directly to the space used can be deducted in full. Other expenses that benefit the entire home must be prorated, based on your business use percentage, as explained on page 76. If you buy shelving or storage cabinets, you'll have to depreciate them under the applicable cost recovery method.

Documenting your storage deductions. In addition to keeping track of your expenses with receipts, bills, statements, and other substantiation, you may want to take some photographs at various times during the year. Take an inventory count periodically and record goods received and shipped. These records will help you prove that the space was used on a regular basis.

Tax$aver Tip. *Keep in mind that it's possible to meet both the home office tests and the rules for inventory storage, resulting in a larger business use percentage and, of course, in a larger deduction. It's a good way to benefit from such underutilized space as an attic, basement, closet, garage, loft, or spare room.* ■

Computer, Educational & Other Business Expenses

Typical business expenses outside salespeople regularly incur include the costs of computer equipment, business-related education, and job hunting, among others. The self-employed can deduct those expenses in full. If you're an employee, however, you must claim unreimbursed business expenses as a miscellaneous deduction on Schedule A. Such expenses are deductible only if you itemize and then only to the extent that the total of all miscellaneous deductions, with a few minor exceptions, exceeds 2% of your adjusted gross income.

Not subject to the limitation are impairment-related work expenses for handicapped employees and certain advance commissions that you repay later (see page 16).

Tax$aver Tip. *In light of the new limitations on the deductibility of employee business expenses, it's especially important that you claim every deduction you're entitled to so you can exceed the 2% floor. Know what expenses are deductible and keep careful records to substantiate them.*

Home computers. If computer equipment is located in your home and you use it for both personal and business purposes, you must keep track of both business and personal use during the year in order to arrive at your business use percentage (BUP); this determines how much of the cost of your computer equipment you can deduct. (See page 41 for information about listed property rules as they apply to computers.) A form to compute BUP is on page 129.

In order for an *employee* to claim any deduction for the business use of a home computer, leased or owned, the use must be for the convenience of the employer and be a required purchase or lease as a condition of employment. By all means, obtain a written statement from your employer. It will be helpful to your case if employees in similar jobs are also required to purchase or lease a computer.

When it comes to deducting the cost of computer software, you have three options, but your choice must be consistent from year to year. If the price is low, you can deduct the entire cost in the current year. If the price is high, deduct the cost over a 5-year estimated life or, if you can establish why this is necessary, over a shorter period.

Tax$aver Tip. *When you purchase software used for business at the same time that you buy hardware, have the cost of the software listed separately, unless they're sold as a package. Otherwise, you'll be writing off the software over the same, longer useful life of the hardware.*

Educational expenses. Ordinary and necessary educational expenses related to your job or business are deductible if they meet one of the following conditions:

1. They're required by your employer, or by law or regulations, to keep your salary, status, or job.
2. The course of study maintains or improves skills needed in your job.

Even when you meet the above requirements, you can't deduct the expenses if the education is necessary in order to meet the minimum educational requirements for your business or is part of a program of study that will lead to qualifying you for a new business.

Deductions you can claim are amounts spent for tuition, books, supplies, laboratory fees, correspondence courses, tutoring, and research and typing to prepare a paper. If your educational expenses are deductible, you're also allowed to deduct transportation expenses between your general work area and a school located beyond that area, between where you work and a school within the same general area, and between your home and school if it's not farther than if you traveled from work to school.

To determine your deduction, you can use either the standard mileage rate of 22½¢ per mile or the actual cost method (see page 37). If you're away from home primarily to obtain education, you can deduct the costs of travel, meals, and lodging, but not any expenses for personal activities.

Educational assistance payments received may be tax-exempt; if so, they must be deducted from your educational expenses. Beginning on August 17, 1986, only scholarships for tuition and course-required fees, books, supplies, and equipment for degree candidates are exempt from tax.

When employers provide educational assistance programs to employees under a qualified, separate written plan, the Tax Reform Act of 1986 allows you to exclude from gross income up to $5,250 of amounts paid on your behalf by your employer. Annual amounts that exceed that figure must be included in income. You may not deduct any educational expenses for which you are reimbursed, but you may be able to deduct expenses if they *exceed* the lesser of either the amount reimbursed or $5,250, as long as they meet the other tests for deductibility.

Job-hunting expenses. Amounts you spend for travel, transportation, resumés, and employment agency fees are deductible under the following circumstances:

- You look for a *new* job in your *current* occupation, whether you're successful or not.
- You're unemployed and are looking for the *same* kind of work you did for your last employer, but only if a substantial amount of time has not passed.
- You travel to and from a new area primarily to look for a job in your present occupation.
- You travel looking for a job while in the new area, even though the cost of getting there and back is not deductible.
- You use your car to visit employment agencies and have resumés prepared or distributed.

You may use either the standard mileage rate of 22½¢ per mile or the actual cost method to compute your deduction for auto use. If your employer pays you back for an employment agency fee in a later year, you must include it in income if you previously deducted it. You don't have to include in income any fees paid directly by your employer to the employment agency.

Moving expenses. People in outside sales can deduct job-related moving expenses, whether they're just entering the work force, they were transferred, or they quit and found a new job on their own, as long as they satisfy the time and distance tests. Self-employed people must move for legitimate business reasons to qualify for the deduction. Under the provisions of the Tax Reform Act of 1986, these deductions are now available *only* as itemized deductions, even for the self-employed.

In order to meet the *time test*, employees must work full-time for at least 39 weeks during the first 12 months after arriving at the new job location. Self-employed people must satisfy this same test and also work full-time for at least 78 weeks during the first 24 months after arrival. You can work for more than one employer, and you don't have to work 39 weeks in a row. If you deduct the expenses and later on don't meet the time test, you either amend the prior return or simply include the total amount of your previously claimed moving expense deduction in other income in the year you fail to meet the test.

For married couples who both work, only one has to satisfy the full-time work test if a joint return is filed. Otherwise, each must meet the test.

The time test doesn't have to be met if you're disabled, you're laid off or fired (not for willful misconduct), or you transfer for your employer's benefit.

The *distance test* can best be understood if you complete the following:

1. Enter the number of miles from your *former* home to your *new* principal work place: _____
2. Enter the number of miles from your *former* home to your *former* principal work place: (_____)
3. Subtract line 2 from line 1: _____

If line 3 is 35 miles or more, you've satisfied this test. If it's less, you can't claim *any* moving expense deductions. If you had no former principal place of work, your new job site must be at least 35 miles from your former residence.

Use the shortest route between the locations to figure the distances. Your principal place of work is where you'll spend the most time, where your work is centered, or where you'll work permanently (not temporarily).

Other deductible moving expenses include moving household goods and personal items, travel between your old and new residences, pre-move house-hunting expenses, temporary living expenses, expenses of disposing of your old home and buying your new one, and certain travel by car. For more information on moving expenses and some limitations that may apply, ask for IRS Publication 521: *Moving Expenses.*

Business gifts. The cost of business gifts can be deducted if the value doesn't exceed $25 given directly or indirectly to any one individual during the tax year. Items permanently imprinted with your name and given to numerous business contacts are not subject to the $25 limit if the cost is $4 or less. Gifts given to a retailer, as opposed to an individual, for use on business premises are not subject to the $25 limit.

Health insurance. Under the Tax Reform Act of 1986, the self-employed are allowed to deduct as a business expense 25% of health insurance payments in a taxable year paid for themselves, their spouses, and their dependents. No deduction is allowed to the extent that it exceeds earned income, and the amount deducted can't also be claimed as a medical expense deduction on Schedule A, Form 1040. This deduction is eliminated after 1989. The amount that's deductible is ignored when computing net earnings from self-employment (see page 18).

If you or your spouse is also an employee and eligible to participate in a plan maintained by an employer, you can't claim the 25% deduction as a business expense.

Business telephone calls. If you make many long-distance business calls from your residential phone, total them from your monthly bill, record them in the Business Expense Register on page 101, and deduct them as a business expense.

Other employee expenses. Other deductible expenses include dues to professional societies, medical examinations required by an employer, occupational taxes, the cost of small tools and supplies used in your work (if used up in less than a year), and subscriptions to work-related professional journals and trade magazines.

If you have sub-sales representatives who work for you on a strict commission basis, be sure to keep complete records of sales and commission reports to document the payments. ∎

Casualty damages to your property from cata-strophic or other similar events or thefts of property may be deductible. Before the deduction can be claimed, the amount of the loss and whether or not there was any personal use of the property during the year will have to be determined.

Generally, business property losses are fully deductible regardless of the cause and whether or not you itemize your deductions; they're reduced only by any insurance or other reimbursements you receive or expect to receive.

Casualty Losses

The IRS defines a casualty as "the damage, destruction, or loss of property resulting from an identifiable event that is sudden, unexpected, or unusual." A casualty loss is deductible in the tax year the loss occurs.

Determining the casualty loss amount. Generally, a casualty loss amount is the lesser of either the property's adjusted basis at the time the loss occurred or the decrease in its fair market value (FMV) from immediately before to immediately after the casualty. However, if the property is *completely* destroyed, the deductible loss is the adjusted basis less any salvage value or insurance proceeds or other compensation either received or sure to be recovered. The decline in FMV is ignored.

If the casualty loss involves property used only partially for business, the loss must be divided as if there were two separate occurrences. The personal loss portion is subject to two limitations—the $100 rule and the 10% rule. This means you must reduce the loss by $100, and the total of all such losses during the year must be reduced by 10% of your adjusted gross income.

Examples of deductible losses. For your reference, the following events have been allowed as deductions for property losses and damages:
- Accidents, if unavoidable
- Cleanup expenses

- Earthquakes, earthslides, avalanches, sudden sinking of land
- Explosions, bomb damage, fires, lightning, volcanic eruptions
- Hail, snow, ice storms, blizzards, dust storms, hurricanes, tornadoes, sudden wind damage, smog (if unusual, sudden, or severe)
- Vandalism, looting, riots
- Water rise (if sudden), floods, tidal waves

You must compute the loss for each asset damaged or destroyed separately, even though they may all be part of the same property and were damaged by the same casualty.

Losses from Theft

The IRS defines a theft as ''the unlawful taking and removing of money or property with the intent to deprive the owner of it. You need only show that the theft was illegal under the law of the state where it occurred, and that it was done with criminal intent.'' With few exceptions, property or money which merely disappears or is mislaid is not a theft.

When to deduct. Such losses are deductible only in the year of discovery, which may or may not be the year the theft actually took place. If the year of discovery is over and you haven't filed your return yet, don't claim the loss if you think the property will be recovered; deduct such a loss only when it's clear that recovery will not occur. Then you'll need to prove that you were the owner of the property, that it was actually stolen, when you first discovered the theft, and how you arrived at the dollar amount of the loss.

If any of your property is stolen, contact a law enforcement agency and your insurance company immediately after you discover the theft. For tax purposes, however, it's not required that the police actually investigate the theft.

Determining the theft loss amount. The cost of the property and its FMV at the time of the theft must be determined. As a cost basis, use your original sales contract, purchase orders, sales receipt, or other written proof. Your loss is either the full FMV or its adjusted basis (original cost plus improvements and less depreciation, even if not claimed), whichever is less. If you later recover your property, your loss is either the decline in value from the time it was stolen until the time recovered or the adjusted basis before the theft, whichever is less. You must always reduce your loss by any expected insurance reimbursement, even if it's an estimated amount or is not received until a later tax year.

If the property happened to be used for both business and personal purposes, treat the theft as if there were two separate occurrences (the same as for casualty losses—see page 69).

Supporting Your Claim

As you might expect, there have been many court cases involving casualty and theft losses claimed by taxpayers. Clearly, you must have extensive proof to support your claim.

To record business and personal property losses, use the form provided on page 129. In addition, gather as much written information as soon as possible after the loss occurs, including a statement of the nature and type of loss; copies of insurance, fire, or police reports; proof that you owned the property; and receipts for purchases, additions, or improvements. You should also have appraisals or reports showing how FMV before

and after the loss was determined, photographs of the damage, and receipts for any damage repairs you've completed. If it was a theft, obtain a copy of the police report showing when you learned the property was missing.

Tax$aver Tip. *It's important, and usually relatively easy, to prove the original purchase price of your property. If you don't, the IRS may arbitrarily set the amount, which could reduce your loss dramatically. It's best to investigate all the acceptable methods of valuing your property both before and after the loss, then use the method that gives you the highest value.*

Adjustments to cost basis. Casualty and theft losses decrease the property's basis by the amount of the deductible loss and any insurance or other reimbursements received. Any money spent to repair or restore your property will increase the basis. And if your reimbursements are greater than the basis before the casualty, this excess gain is taxable and added back to basis.

How and where to report. To report casualty or theft losses, transfer the information on page 129 to Form 4684; use Section B for investment casualty and theft losses, Section A for any personal portion. In certain situations, you may also need to complete Form 4797.

Tax$aver Tip. *If the amounts claimed for losses are large, attach complete documentation directly to your return to help avoid an audit.*

Publication 549 is available from the IRS if you need more detailed information on this subject. ■

Logs & Registers

Record Keeping Made Easy

The various logs and registers you'll need to keep track of your deductible expenses throughout the year, as well as forms to help you compute your allowable deductions, are explained in this section.

Auto, Computer & Other Property Cost, Basis & Depreciation Information (page 82). Use this form to record the cost basis of your home, major purchases with a useful life of more than a year, and permanent additions or improvements to your property that either increase its value or prolong its useful life.

Unless you're very knowledgeable, have your tax advisor compute your total current allowable depreciation deduction on this form. Record any home office depreciation subject to allocation for business use on the Computation of Business Use Expenses form on page 127. For more information on depreciation, see page 40.

Permanent Recurring Mileage Record (page 83). Use this form to reduce the time you spend entering odometer readings for trips (including those away from home) you make on a regular basis, even your daily commute. Simply record the odometer readings one time, note the location and purpose, and check "one way" or "round trip." Then assign a code, such as A, B, etc., to each trip. For subsequent trips, just use the Log of Recurring Trips.

Log of Recurring Trips (page 84). Record recurring trips in this log, using the information from the permanent record. When recording the dates, choose a time period that's most suitable for the particular trip. Or enter the beginning date and wait until the space is filled before entering the ending date; then just start over on a new line.

In the column "Ongoing Count or Dates," enter either a mark for each trip for this code or just the date. Enter the total number of trips for that period in the next column. Then simply multiply by the number of miles to arrive at a total and distribute the total in the proper column.

Log of Nonrecurring Trips (page 89). Use this log for nonregular auto use, entering the information for each trip, even those away from home. Though you can maintain this log on a weekly basis, you'll need to keep track of the date, destination, and odometer readings for each trip as it occurs.

Commissions, Advances & Reimbursements Received (page 97). On this form you can record all the payments you receive during the year. Be sure to identify the type of payment—commission, advance, or reimbursement.

Commissions Earned & Not Paid (page 99). Use this form to help you keep track of large orders you've completed but for which you have not yet received payment.

Business Expense Register (page 101). Use this register to record, categorize, and total all your business expenses, regardless of the method of payment. Be sure to stay up to date by making entries on a regular basis.

For each payment by check, simply list the requested information. It's wise to maintain a separate checking account for all your business expenses.

For payments by credit card, either enter each expense as incurred or wait until you receive your monthly statement, write one check, and distribute the expenses to the proper columns.

For payments that don't fit the column headings provided, label and use blank columns for frequently made payments and the "Miscellaneous Expenses" column for nonrecurring ones.

Tax$aver Tips. *Pay all bills for deductible expenses before year-end so they'll be deductible that year. Note that the law allows you to deduct credit card charges in the year incurred, even if payment occurs the following year.*

Don't lump large amounts into such categories as "other expenses" or "miscellaneous." Instead, identify large amounts separately and combine smaller amounts under one heading.

Away-from-Home Business Expense Log (page 110). In order to establish that the trip was an ordinary and necessary business expense, you'll need to indicate the date of departure and return and the business purpose. (Be sure the mileage is recorded on one of the mileage logs if the trip was by car.)

To fully substantiate away-from-home business expenses, you must also obtain and save receipts, itemized bills or statements, canceled checks, and other such documentary evidence for all lodging expenses, regardless of the amount spent, and for other expenditures of $25 or more (not including tips).

Since under the provisions of the Tax Reform Act of 1986 entertainment expenses must now be reduced by 20%, such expenses are reported separately, even when they're incurred away from home.

Record items you charge to your employer (by credit card or otherwise), but not any amounts your employer pays for directly.

Summary of Out-of-Pocket Expenses Paid in Cash (page 120).

Here you can periodically summarize typical out-of-pocket expenses paid in cash. (Use a diary or tape recorder to record them and always get receipts when possible.) Record the totals in the Business Expense Register, filling in the appropriate columns, or write yourself a check.

Actual Cost Method/Standard Mileage Rate (page 121).

Once you've accumulated all your auto expenses for the year, compute your total auto deduction on this form, using both the actual cost method and the standard mileage rate. Claim the amount that gives you the greatest deduction.

Entertainment Expense Log (page 122). Use this log to record all your business entertainment expenses, whether they're incurred away from home, in a local restaurant, or in your home. Be sure the information is complete. You can use the approved IRS rate of 22½¢ per mile for an auto used for entertainment purposes. Transportation costs for entertainment, regardless of the mode, do not have to be reduced by 20%.

Computation of Business Use Percentages (BUP) (page 127). If you use a portion of your home for business, the IRS allows you to determine the expenses allocable to the business portion by any reasonable method. Generally, however, only two

methods are used (the form has space for figuring percentages using both methods).

For the *room-by-room* method, you divide the number of rooms, or fractions thereof, used for business by the total number of rooms in your home. (Use this method only if the rooms are comparable in size; do *not* include utility rooms or the bathrooms in the count.) If, for example, you use 1½ rooms of a 6-room house for business, your BUP would be 25%.

For the *square-footage* method, you need to know the square footage both for the space used for business and for the entire home. Include all entryways, hallways, storage areas, closets, utility rooms, and bathrooms.

Once you've figured the total space used for business, divide it by the total square feet of your home to arrive at your BUP.

Computation of Business Use Expenses (page 127).

Expenses of operating your home fall into one of three categories. They can be business or direct expenses deductible in full, indirect expenses that are partially deductible, or expenses completely unrelated to business and not deductible at all.

Expenses deductible in full are called *direct* expenses by the IRS since they benefit only the part of your home used for business. (Decorating and making repairs to the space used are examples.) Though typically fully deductible, all direct expenses are still subject to the deduction limitation discussed on page 78.

Partially deductible expenses are referred to as *indirect* expenses by the IRS since they benefit the entire home, not just the personal or business portion. Only the business portion of these expenses is deductible (you do this by applying your BUP against the amounts paid).

You can never claim a deduction equal to the fair rental value of the business portion of your home; nor can you claim deductions for landscaping, lawn care, or repairs to personal areas.

Record deductible expenses in the Business Expense Register; label each amount either (D) for direct or (I) for indirect. Total each type of expense, transfer the totals to this form, and make the necessary computations to arrive at your total deductions *before* considering the limitations.

Computation of Deduction Limitations on Home Office Use (page 128). The primary purpose of the limitation is to prevent indirect expenses resulting from the business use of your home from *creating* or *increasing* a net business loss. The form is designed to help you determine if any of the limitation levels apply to you. Depending on the amount of your net, not gross, income (effective 1987), you may be able to deduct all, some, or none of your direct, indirect, and depreciation expenses. Mortgage interest, real estate taxes, and casualty losses are always deductible on Schedule A if you itemize.

To determine gross income, the starting point in applying the limitations, you may include only income from qualifying business use derived from the business use of your home.

To determine net income, as now required, subtract from gross income all trade or business expenses not subject to allocation or limitation (see facing page). Then deduct your remaining expenses from net income in the order shown on the form. As you complete the form, you'll quickly discover if any of the three categories of deduc-

tions are either limited or deductible in full. Beginning in 1987, the new law allows home office deductions disallowed solely because of the income limitation to be carried forward to later years (also subject to limitation).

Keep in mind that even if the limitation rules restrict or eliminate your deductions for direct and indirect expenses, you can still deduct with no restrictions any ordinary and necessary business expenses that do not relate to the business use of your home.

Computation of BUP for Computer Equipment (page 129). Use this form to calculate your business use percentage for any computer equipment used in your trade or business.

Summary of All Expenses (page 130). Here you can summarize your expenses for the year so that you or your tax advisor can easily transfer the totals directly to Form 2106 or Schedule C.

Outside Sales Deduction Checklist

The following list summarizes the deductible expenses someone in outside sales might incur.

Refer to this list often to be sure you're not overlooking any deductible expenses.

Automobile Expenses

Air conditioners*
Alarm systems*, theft prevention kits
Auto club membership fees and dues
Auto repair books and manuals, maps
Carpets, floor mats, upholstery
Chauffeurs' salaries and licenses
Convertible tops*, boots*, sunroofs*, covers
Emergency repair kits, road lights, safety
    flares, safety belts
Headlights, fog lights, flashlights, mirrors
Installation costs*
Insurance, license and registration fees
Interest on auto loan or gas credit card
Job-hunting miles driven
Loss on sale of car
Luggage racks and carriers*
Moving expense miles driven
Radios*, stereos*, speakers*, tape players*,
    CB antennas, cellular phones*, clocks
Rebuilt engines*
Smog and diagnostic inspections

Tow bars*, roll bars*
Windshield washers, fluids, wiper arms and
    blades
Wire wheels*, mags*, rims, wheel balancing
    and alignment

Direct Expenses of Home Office Subject to Limitation

Carpets*, drapes*, throw rugs, cleaning
Installation costs*
Painting, redecorating, and repairs of
    business space

Indirect Expenses of Home Office Subject to Allocation and Limitation

Alarm system for theft prevention*
Casualty losses
Central air conditioning or heating system*
Interest on mortgage, points paid
Real estate taxes
Repairs, maintenance, improvements*
Utility fees

Fully Deductible Business Expenses

Air conditioner (portable)*, fans,
    dehumidifier for computer equipment*
Bookcases and shelving, built-in*

79

Books**, technical references**, professional
or trade journals**, subscriptions**
Credit and collection expenses
Delivery
Dues**, memberships**
Employment-related education**
Entertainment at home for business
Furniture and equipment rental or lease
Interest on business loans, credit cards, bank
service charges
Job-hunting expenses**, resumés**, employ-
ment agency fees*
Legal and professional services**
Licenses and taxes**
Loss on disposition of business assets
Medical exam required by employer
Pictures, lamps, mirrors, clocks
Salaries and wages of employees, outside ser-
vices, casual labor
Seminars (but not for investment purposes)
Tax$aver series**
Telephones*, answering machines*, message
or secretarial services

Typewriters*, calculators*, adding machines*
Video camera and recorder*
* May have to depreciate
**Not subject to convenience of employer test

Claiming Deductions on Your Return

Outside salespeople who are employees continue
to report their business expenses on Form 2106.
But effective in 1987, you deduct any expenses
that exceed reimbursements only as a miscellaneous deduction on Schedule A; this deduction is
limited to the amount that exceeds 2% of your
adjusted gross income.

Self-employed outside salespeople who are
sole owners of a business use Schedule C, Form
1040—Profit or (Loss) From Business or Profes-
sion. If the business is a partnership, use Form
1065. Complete Form 1120 if your business is
incorporated. ■

Record of Important Information & Dates

Personal Information

Name_____ Address _____

City _____ State _____ Zip _____

Telephone: Home _____ Business _____

Automobile Information

Odometer Reading Jan. 1, 19___ _____ Dec. 31, 19___ _____

Year & Make _____ Model _____

Vehicle ID No. _____ Vehicle Weight_____ Lbs.

Engine Serial No. _____ Color _____

Recommended Fuel _____ Oil Weight & Grade _____

Tire Size _____ Recommended Pressure _____

Capacities: Coolant _____

    Fuel _____ Oil/Filter No. _____

    Transmission _____ Radiator _____

Licensing Information

State License Plate No. _____ Expiration Date _____

State Driver's License No. _____ Expiration Date _____

Oil Company Credit Card Information

Card Issued by	Account Number	Expiration Date

Insurance Information

Company _____ Telephone _____

Agent _____ Telephone _____

Policy Number _____ Annual Premium _____

Loss Payable Clause to _____ Term _____ to _____

Liability		Collision & Comprehensive	
Coverage	Limits	Coverage	Limits

Business Use Percentage

Year	Home Office	Automobile	Home Computer
Current 19__			
Prior 19__			
2nd Prior 19__			

Important ID Numbers & Dates

Description	Number	Expiration Date or Payment Due
Federal Business ID No.		
Auto Loan/Lease Payment		
State & Local Business Licenses		
State & Local Property Taxes		

Auto, Computer & Other Property Cost, Basis & Depreciation Information

Date Acq'd. or Placed in Service	If Car, Mileage at Start	Description of Property & Major Additions	Class of Property or Recovery %	Recovery Period in Years	Method Accel. or Straight Line	Cost			Total Depreciation in All Prior Years (D)	Unrecovered Cost at Start of Year (C) Less (D) (E)	Depreciation This Year (F)	Unrecovered Cost at End of Year (E) Less (F)
						Original or Other Basis (A)	Basis Adjustments Sec. 179 or ITC (B)	Cost Basis for Depreciation (A) Less (B) (C)				

Note: Investment tax credit claimed on property before 1986 may be subject to recapture when sold or traded. Depreciation computed on form is subject to certain limitations and may be further reduced by application of business use percentage. For more information on depreciation, see page 40.

Permanent Recurring Mileage Record

Code	From/to & Business Purpose or Benefit Expected or Received	Odometer			Check		Code	From/to & Business Purpose or Benefit Expected or Received	Odometer			Check	
		Depart	Arrive	Miles Each Trip	One Way	R/T			Depart	Arrive	Miles Each Trip	One Way	R/T
A	Home to office commute	9,086	9,138	52		✓							
B	Office to XYZ Co. Customer	10,641	10,715	74		✓							

Log of Recurring Trips

Inclusive Dates	Code	Miles Each Trip (A)	Total Repeat Mileage for Period			Miles Driven (A) × (B)	Distribution of Miles Driven in Period					
			Number of Trips in Period				Trade or Business	Investment	Commuting			
			Ongoing Count or Dates	Total(B)								
1/1 to 1/31	A	26	⊥HH ⊥HH III	13		338			338			
1/1 to 1/15	B	74	1/5, 1/7, 1/9, 1/10 1/12, 1/14	6		444	444					
to												
to												
to												
to												
to												
to												
to												
to												
to												
to												
to												
to												
to												
Note: See page 74 for instructions.			**Subtotals**									

84

Log of Recurring Trips

| Inclusive Dates | Total Repeat Mileage for Period | | | | | Distribution of Miles Driven in Period | | | | | |
| | Code | Miles Each Trip (A) | Number of Trips in Period | | Miles Driven (A) × (B) | Trade or Business | Investment | Commuting | | | |
			Ongoing Count or Dates	Total(B)							
to											
to											
to											
to											
to											
to											
to											
to											
to											
to											
to											
to											
to											
to											
to											
Note: See page 74 for instructions.			**Subtotals**								

Log of Recurring Trips

| Inclusive Dates | Total Repeat Mileage for Period | | | | | | Distribution of Miles Driven in Period | | | | | |
| | Code | Miles Each Trip (A) | Number of Trips in Period | | Miles Driven (A) × (B) | Trade or Business | Investment | Commuting | | | | |
			Ongoing Count or Dates	Total(B)								
to												
to												
to												
to												
to												
to												
to												
to												
to												
to												
to												
to												
to												
to												
to												
Note: See page 74 for instructions.			**Subtotals**									

Log of Recurring Trips

Inclusive Dates	Code	Miles Each Trip (A)	Number of Trips in Period — Ongoing Count or Dates	Total(B)	Miles Driven (A) × (B)	Trade or Business	Investment	Commuting			
			Total Repeat Mileage for Period			**Distribution of Miles Driven in Period**					
to											
to											
to											
to											
to											
to											
to											
to											
to											
to											
to											
to											
to											
to											
to											
Note: See page 74 for instructions.			**Subtotals**								

Log of Recurring Trips

Inclusive Dates	Total Repeat Mileage for Period					Distribution of Miles Driven in Period					
	Code	Miles Each Trip (A)	Number of Trips in Period		Miles Driven (A) × (B)	Trade or Business	Investment	Commuting			
			Ongoing Count or Dates	Total(B)							
to											
to											
to											
to											
to											
to											
to											
to											
to											
to											
to											
to											
to											
to											
to											
Note: See page 74 for instructions.			**Totals for Year**								

Log of Nonrecurring Trips

Date 19 __	From/to	Business Purpose or Benefit Expected or Received	Odometer			Details of Miles Driven					
			Depart	Arrive	Miles This Trip	Trade or Business	Invest-ment				
1/6	Office to Bishop Co. R/T	Prospective client	10,778	10,862	84	84					
1/7	Office to Plaza R/T	Dinner with R. Little, prev. TPI, re product	10,981	10,999	18	18					
Note: Odometer readings are sufficient for round-trips but are not necessary for in-between stops. See page 75 for instructions.		Subtotals									

Log of Nonrecurring Trips

Date 19 __	From/to	Business Purpose or Benefit Expected or Received	Odometer			Details of Miles Driven					
			Depart	Arrive	Miles This Trip	Trade or Business	Invest-ment				
Note: Odometer readings are sufficient for round-trips but are not necessary for in-between stops. See page 75 for instructions.			**Subtotals**								

Log of Nonrecurring Trips

Date 19 __	From/to	Business Purpose or Benefit Expected or Received	Odometer			Details of Miles Driven					
			Depart	Arrive	Miles This Trip	Trade or Business	Invest- ment				
Note: Odometer readings are sufficient for round-trips but are not necessary for in-between stops. See page 75 for instructions.		Subtotals									

Log of Nonrecurring Trips

Date 19 __	From/to	Business Purpose or Benefit Expected or Received	Odometer			Details of Miles Driven					
			Depart	Arrive	Miles This Trip	Trade or Business	Invest-ment				
Note: Odometer readings are sufficient for round-trips but are not necessary for in-between stops. See page 75 for instructions.			**Subtotals**								

Log of Nonrecurring Trips

Date 19 __	From/to	Business Purpose or Benefit Expected or Received	Odometer			Details of Miles Driven					
			Depart	Arrive	Miles This Trip	Trade or Business	Invest-ment				
Note: Odometer readings are sufficient for round-trips but are not necessary for in-between stops. See page 75 for instructions.		**Subtotals**									

Log of Nonrecurring Trips

Date 19 __	From/to	Business Purpose or Benefit Expected or Received	Odometer			Details of Miles Driven					
			Depart	Arrive	Miles This Trip	Trade or Business	Invest-ment				
Note: Odometer readings are sufficient for round-trips but are not necessary for in-between stops. See page 75 for instructions.			**Subtotals**								

Log of Nonrecurring Trips

Date 19 __	From/to	Business Purpose or Benefit Expected or Received	Odometer			Details of Miles Driven					
			Depart	Arrive	Miles This Trip	Trade or Business	Invest-ment				
Note: Odometer readings are sufficient for round-trips but are not necessary for in-between stops. See page 75 for instructions.			**Subtotals**								

Log of Nonrecurring Trips

Date 19 __	From/to	Business Purpose or Benefit Expected or Received	Odometer			Details of Miles Driven					
			Depart	Arrive	Miles This Trip	Trade or Business	Invest-ment				
Note: Odometer readings are sufficient for round-trips but are not necessary for in-between stops. See page 75 for instructions.			**Totals for Year**								

Commissions, Advances & Reimbursements Received

Paym't. Rec'd.	Dates For Earnings From	To	Description of Payment Commission (C), Advance (A), Reimbursement (R)		Amount Received		Paym't. Rec'd.	Dates For Earnings From	To	Description of Payment Commission (C), Advance (A), Reimbursement (R)		Amount Received	
1/5	12/1	12/31	Reg. Commission ck.	C	$4,187	56							
										Subtotal			

Commissions, Advances & Reimbursements Received

Dates			Description of Payment				Amount Received	Dates			Description of Payment			Amount Received
Paym't. Rec'd.	For Earnings		Commission (C), Advance (A), Reimbursement (R)					Paym't. Rec'd.	For Earnings		Commission (C), Advance (A), Reimbursement (R)			
	From	To							From	To				
								Total Payments Received for Year						
								Recap: Commissions					(C)	
								Advances					(A)	
								Reimbursements					(R)	
								Totals						

98

Commissions Earned & Not Paid

Date of Order	Customer	Total Sale		Commission Due		Date of Order	Customer	Total Sale		Commission Due	

Commissions Earned & Not Paid

Date of Order	Customer	Total Sale	Commission Due	Date of Order	Customer	Total Sale	Commission Due

Business Expense Register

Date 19___	Paid to/Description	Check #, Cash, or Cr. Card	Auto Expenses	Rent or Home Office Expenses	Utilities & Telephone	Office & Operating Supplies	Dues & Publi-cations			Miscellaneous Expenses	
										Description	Amount
1/19	Cash expenses 1/1 – 1/15	Cash	17 53	(D) 35 00	9 80	8 91				Entertainment	37 65
Note: See page 75 for instructions.		Subtotals									

Business Expense Register

Date 19___	Paid to/Description	Check #, Cash, or Cr. Card	Auto Expenses	Rent or Home Office Expenses	Utilities & Telephone	Office & Operating Supplies	Dues & Publi-cations			Miscellaneous Expenses	
										Description	Amount
Note: See page 75 for instructions.		Subtotals									

102

Business Expense Register

Date 19__	Paid to/Description	Check #, Cash, or Cr. Card	Auto Expenses	Rent or Home Office Expenses	Utilities & Telephone	Office & Operating Supplies	Dues & Publi-cations			Miscellaneous Expenses	
										Description	Amount
Note: See page 75 for instructions.		Subtotals									

Business Expense Register

Date 19___	Paid to/Description	Check #, Cash, or Cr. Card	Auto Expenses	Rent or Home Office Expenses	Utilities & Telephone	Office & Operating Supplies	Dues & Publi-cations			Miscellaneous Expenses	
										Description	Amount
Note: See page 75 for instructions.		**Subtotals**									

Business Expense Register

Date 19___	Paid to/Description	Check #, Cash, or Cr. Card	Auto Expenses	Rent or Home Office Expenses	Utilities & Telephone	Office & Operating Supplies	Dues & Publi-cations			Miscellaneous Expenses	
										Description	Amount
Note: See page 75 for instructions.		Subtotals									

105

Business Expense Register

Date 19___	Paid to/Description	Check #, Cash, or Cr. Card	Auto Expenses		Rent or Home Office Expenses		Utilities & Telephone		Office & Operating Supplies		Dues & Publi-cations						Miscellaneous Expenses		
																		Description	Amount	
Note: See page 75 for instructions.		**Subtotals**																		

Business Expense Register

Date 19___	Paid to/Description	Check #, Cash, or Cr. Card	Auto Expenses		Rent or Home Office Expenses	Utilities & Telephone	Office & Operating Supplies	Dues & Publi-cations				Miscellaneous Expenses	
												Description	Amount
Note: See page 75 for instructions.		Subtotals											

Business Expense Register

Date 19___	Paid to/Description	Check #, Cash, or Cr. Card	Auto Expenses	Rent or Home Office Expenses	Utilities & Telephone	Office & Operating Supplies	Dues & Publi-cations			Miscellaneous Expenses	
										Description	Amount
Note: See page 75 for instructions.		**Subtotals**									

108

Business Expense Register

Date 19___	Paid to/Description	Check #, Cash, or Cr. Card	Auto Expenses	Rent or Home Office Expenses	Utilities & Telephone	Office & Operating Supplies	Dues & Publi- cations			Miscellaneous Expenses	
										Description	Amount
	Totals										

Away-from-Home Business Expense Log

Date of Trip 19__	Total Days Away on Bus.	Destination	Business Purpose or Nature of Benefit Expected or Received	Travel & Transportation Costs	Auto Use or Rental Gas & Oil	Lodging	Meals		Incidental Expenses				Totals
									Parking & Tolls	Bus & Taxi	Phone Calls		
1/5–1/6	1	LA	Sales calls	98 00	63 60	92 81	62 88		6 75		1 80		325 84
Note: Indicate whether payment is cash (c), check (ck), or credit card (cc).			Subtotals										

Away-from-Home Business Expense Log

Date of Trip 19__	Total Days Away on Bus.	Destination	Business Purpose or Nature of Benefit Expected or Received	Travel & Trans-portation Costs	Auto Use or Rental Gas & Oil	Lodging	Meals		Incidental Expenses				Totals
									Parking & Tolls	Bus & Taxi	Phone Calls		
Note: Indicate whether payment is cash (c), check (ck), or credit card (cc).		**Subtotals**											

Away-from-Home Business Expense Log

Date of Trip 19___	Total Days Away on Bus.	Destination	Business Purpose or Nature of Benefit Expected or Received	Travel & Trans-portation Costs	Auto Use or Rental Gas & Oil		Lodging		Meals			Incidental Expenses						Totals	
												Parking & Tolls		Bus & Taxi		Phone Calls			
Note: Indicate whether payment is cash (c), check (ck), or credit card (cc).		**Subtotals**																	

Away-from-Home Business Expense Log

Date of Trip 19__	Total Days Away on Bus.	Destination	Business Purpose or Nature of Benefit Expected or Received	Travel & Trans- portation Costs	Auto Use or Rental Gas & Oil	Lodging	Meals		Incidental Expenses					Totals
									Parking & Tolls	Bus & Taxi	Phone Calls			
Note: Indicate whether payment is cash (c), check (ck), or credit card (cc).			**Subtotals**											

Away-from-Home Business Expense Log

Date of Trip 19__	Total Days Away on Bus.	Destination	Business Purpose or Nature of Benefit Expected or Received	Travel & Transportation Costs	Auto Use or Rental Gas & Oil	Lodging	Meals		Incidental Expenses					Totals
									Parking & Tolls	Bus & Taxi	Phone Calls			
Note: Indicate whether payment is cash (c), check (ck), or credit card (cc).		**Subtotals**												

114

Away-from-Home Business Expense Log

Date of Trip 19__	Total Days Away on Bus.	Destination	Business Purpose or Nature of Benefit Expected or Received	Travel & Transportation Costs	Auto Use or Rental / Gas & Oil	Lodging	Meals		Incidental Expenses				Totals
									Parking & Tolls	Bus & Taxi	Phone Calls		
Note: Indicate whether payment is cash (c), check (ck), or credit card (cc).		**Subtotals**											

Away-from-Home Business Expense Log

Date of Trip 19__	Total Days Away on Bus.	Destination	Business Purpose or Nature of Benefit Expected or Received	Travel & Transportation Costs	Auto Use or Rental Gas & Oil	Lodging	Meals		Incidental Expenses				Totals
									Parking & Tolls	Bus & Taxi	Phone Calls		
Note: Indicate whether payment is cash (c), check (ck), or credit card (cc).		**Subtotals**											

116

Away-from-Home Business Expense Log

Date of Trip 19___	Total Days Away on Bus.	Destination	Business Purpose or Nature of Benefit Expected or Received	Travel & Transportation Costs	Auto Use or Rental Gas & Oil	Lodging	Meals		Incidental Expenses				Totals
									Parking & Tolls	Bus & Taxi	Phone Calls		
Note: Indicate whether payment is cash (c), check (ck), or credit card (cc).		**Subtotals**											

Away-from-Home Business Expense Log

Date of Trip 19__	Total Days Away on Bus.	Destination	Business Purpose or Nature of Benefit Expected or Received	Travel & Transportation Costs	Auto Use or Rental Gas & Oil	Lodging	Meals		Incidental Expenses				Totals
									Parking & Tolls	Bus & Taxi	Phone Calls		
Note: Indicate whether payment is cash (c), check (ck), or credit card (cc).		**Subtotals**											

Away-from-Home Business Expense Log

Date of Trip 19__	Total Days Away on Bus.	Destination	Business Purpose or Nature of Benefit Expected or Received	Travel & Trans- portation Costs	Auto Use or Rental Gas & Oil	Lodging	Meals		Incidental Expenses				Totals
									Parking & Tolls	Bus & Taxi	Phone Calls		
Note: Indicate whether payment is cash (c), check (ck), or credit card (cc).		**Totals**											

Summary of Out-of-Pocket Expenses Paid in Cash

Description of Expense	From 1/1 to 1/15	From to	From to	From to	From to	From to	From to	From to	From to	From to	From to	From to	From to
Office Supplies	8 91												
Office Repairs	20 00												
Cleaning Service	15 00												
Entertainment	37 65												
Pay Telephone Calls	9 80												
Gas, Oil, Lube	17 53												
Parking Fees & Tolls	—												
Taxi, Bus & Train Fares	—												
Totals	108 89												
Date Entered in Expense Register	1/19												

Actual Cost Method	Standard Mileage Rate

Actual Cost Method

Computation of Business Use Percentages

Computation for Meeting 50% Test		
Total Miles Driven for Qualified Trade or Business	(A)	
Total Miles Driven for All Purposes during Year	(B)	
Qualified Business Use Percentage (A) ÷ (B)	(C)	%
Computation for Calculating Basis & Deductions		
Qualified Trade or Business Miles	(A)	
Total Miles Driven for Investment/Production of Income	(D)	
Total Business/Invest./Prod. of Income Miles (A) + (D)	(E)	
BUP for Calculating Basis & Deductions (E) ÷ (B)	(F)	%

Computation of Total Auto Deduction

Total Automobile Expenses Subject to Allocation X	(F)	$
Business Parking Fees & Tolls (Deductible in Full)		
Total Auto Deduction for Year 19 _____		$

Note: See page 38 for more information on the actual cost method.

Standard Mileage Rate

Computation of Business Use Percentage

Total Business/Investment/Production of Income Miles	(E)	
Total Miles Driven for All Purposes during Year	(B)	
Business Use Percentage (E) ÷ (B)	(G)	%

Computation of Total Auto Deduction

Multiply (E) or 15,000 Miles (Whichever is Smaller) by 22½¢	$	
Multiply Excess of (E) over 15,000 Miles by 11¢		
For Autos Considered Fully Depreciated, Multiply (E) by 11¢		
Partially Deductible Expenses		
Multiply Interest on Auto Loan by (G) (Limited for Employees)		
Multiply Personal Property Taxes (Where Applicable) by (G)		
Fully Deductible Expenses		
Business Parking Fees & Tolls		
Other Expenses (Where Applicable)		
Total Auto Deduction for Year 19_____	$	

Note: See page 37 for more information on the standard mileage rate.

Entertainment Expense Log

Date 19___	Place & Duration of Entertainment	Who Discussed Business & Was Entertained/ Company, Title, or Occupation	Nature of Discussion & Business Purpose or Benefit Expected or Received	Food & Beverages		Entertain-ment		Tips		Auto Use, Parking & Tolls					
1/4	Plaza 2½ hrs.	D. Hayes, pres. CRC Co. Customer	New product intro	41	50	16	00	10	00	6	00				
Note: See page 54 for information on deducting entertainment expenses.			**Subtotals**												

122

Entertainment Expense Log

Date 19___	Place & Duration of Entertainment	Who Discussed Business & Was Entertained/ Company, Title, or Occupation	Nature of Discussion & Business Purpose or Benefit Expected or Received	Food & Beverages		Entertain-ment		Tips		Auto Use, Parking & Tolls					
Note: See page 54 for information on deducting entertainment expenses.			**Subtotals**												

123

Entertainment Expense Log

Date 19___	Place & Duration of Entertainment	Who Discussed Business & Was Entertained/ Company, Title, or Occupation	Nature of Discussion & Business Purpose or Benefit Expected or Received	Food & Beverages		Entertain- ment		Tips		Auto Use, Parking & Tolls					

Note: See page 54 for information on deducting entertainment expenses.	Subtotals										

Entertainment Expense Log

Date 19___	Place & Duration of Entertainment	Who Discussed Business & Was Entertained/ Company, Title, or Occupation	Nature of Discussion & Business Purpose or Benefit Expected or Received	Food & Beverages	Entertain-ment	Tips	Auto Use, Parking & Tolls		
Note: See page 54 for information on deducting entertainment expenses.			**Subtotals**						

Entertainment Expense Log

Date 19___	Place & Duration of Entertainment	Who Discussed Business & Was Entertained/ Company, Title, or Occupation	Nature of Discussion & Business Purpose or Benefit Expected or Received	Food & Beverages		Entertain-ment		Tips		Auto Use, Parking & Tolls					
Note: See page 54 for information on deducting entertainment expenses.			**Totals for Year**												

Computation of Business Use Percentages	Computation of Business Use Expenses

By Room

Number of Rooms Used for Business . . . .(A)		
Total Rooms Exclusive of Utility & Bathrooms . . . .(B)		
Business Use Percentage (A) ÷ (B) . . . .(C)		%

By Square Footage

Rooms & Areas	Measurements	Total Square Feet	Sq. Ft. Used for Business
Totals for Entire Home & Business Space			
Business Use Percentage (Bus. Sq. Ft. ÷ Total Sq. Ft.) (D)			%

Expenses per Home Office Column of Business Expense Register

Indirect Expenses Subject to Allocation

Mortgage Interest or Rent	$	
Real Estate Taxes		
Utilities & Other Services		
Insurance for One Year		
Repairs That Benefit Entire Home		
Depreciation Expense		
Total Indirect Expenses Subject to Allocation	$	
Multiply by BUP (C) or (D)	×	%
Total Indirect Expenses (H)	$	

Direct Expenses Deductible in Full

Repairs to Business Part of Home	$	
Painting Business Part of Home		
Other Direct Expenses		
Total Direct Expenses (I)	$	
Total Expenses Subject to Limitation (H) + (I) (J)	$	

Computation of Deduction Limitations on Home Office Use

Net Income from Business Activities . . . . (A)	$	

Less

Mortgage Interest ($ X % BUP)	(	)
Real Estate Taxes ($ X % BUP)	(	)
Casualty Losses ($ X % BUP)	(	)
Amount Allowable to Deduct (Total of 3 Prior Lines) . . . . (B)		
Amount Deducted, Lesser of (A) or (B) . . . . (C)	(	)
Limit on Further Deductions, (A) Less (C). If Zero, Stop Here . . . . (D)		

Less Direct & Indirect Expenses Other Than Depreciation (See Page 127)

Direct Expenses	(	)
Indirect Expenses (Reduced by Depreciation Expense Amount)	(	)
Amount Allowable to Deduct (Total of 2 Prior Lines) . . . . (E)		
Amount Deducted, Lesser of (D) or (E) . . . . (F)	(	)
Limit on Depreciation Deduction, (D) Less (F). If Zero, Stop Here . . . . (G)		
Less Depreciation Expense on Business Part of Home ($ X % BUP)	(	)
Amount Allowable to Deduct . . . . (H)		
Amount Deducted, Lesser of (G) or (H) . . . . (I)	$	

Computation of BUP for Computer Equipment

Computation for Meeting 50% Test	Actual	Example
Total Hours Used for Qualified Trade or Business . . . . (A)		810
Total Hours Used for All Purposes during Year . . . . (B)		1,225
BUP for 50% Test (A) ÷ (B) . . . . (C)	%	66.1%
Computation for Calculating Basis & Depreciation		
Total Hours Used for Investment or Income-Producing Purposes . . . . (D)		150
Total Hours Used for Business/Investment (A) + (D) . . . . (E)		960
BUP for Basis & Depreciation (E) ÷ (B) . . . . (F)	%	78.4%

Casualty & Theft Loss Information

Description of Property & Loss Where Located	Date		1 Cost or Other Basis	2 Deprec. Allowed or Allowable	3 Salvage Value if Totally Destroyed	4 Adjusted Basis 1 − (2+3)	5 Reimb. Received or Expected	6 Gain, if Applic. (5) − (4)	Fair Market Value			Loss (Lesser of 4 or 9, and Less 5)
	Acquired	Loss or Discovery							7 Before Loss	8 After Loss	9 Decrease (7)−(8)	

Summary of All Expenses for 19 _____

Source of Information in Your *Tax$aver*	Form 2106		Schedule C	
	Line	Amount	Line	Amount
Business Expense Register (Page 109)				
Auto Gas, Oil, Lube, Repairs, Supplies, Insurance, etc.				
Rent or Home Office Expenses (Direct $_____ Indirect $_____)				
Utilities $_____ & Business Telephone $_____				
Office & Operating Supplies				
Dues & Publications				
_____				
_____				
_____				
Away-from-Home Business Expense Log (Page 119)				
Travel & Transportation Costs, Including Auto Use				
Lodging				
Meals Subject to 80% Rule				
Incidental Expense Totals				
_____				
_____				
Entertainment Expense Log (Page 126)				
Business Meals, Entertainment & Tips Subject to 80% Rule				
Auto Use, Parking & Tolls Not Subject to 80% Rule				
Depreciation Expense Claimed This Year (Page 82)				
Section 179 Deduction (If Elected)				

Tax Help

Choosing & Working with a Tax Advisor

Because of the recent changes in the tax law, it's expected that almost half of all taxpayers will hire a tax advisor to prepare their returns. Even taxpayers who complete their own returns may need the help and advice of a professional tax advisor to solve a particular problem, to prepare for an IRS audit, or to plan for the future. In either case, you'll want to choose a qualified advisor you can trust and work with comfortably and confidently.

Who can be a tax advisor? There are more than 20,000 accounting firms in the U.S. and many thousands of people called tax preparers. Only a handful of states require tax preparers to take classes or be licensed.

It's best to retain someone who can legally represent you at all IRS levels. Generally, this person will be a CPA, an attorney, or an "enrolled agent." All enrolled agents have either worked for the IRS as a revenue agent for 5 years or have passed a demanding 2-day IRS test. Unenrolled tax preparers may represent their clients *only* at the examination level.

Only CPAs, attorneys, and enrolled agents may perform the following:
1. Execute claims for a refund
2. Receive checks in payment of any refund of taxes, penalties, or interest
3. Execute consents to extend the statutory period for assessment or collection of a tax
4. Execute closing agreements with respect to a tax liability or specific matter
5. Delegate authority or substitute another representative

Fees for these services are generally deductible, but now employees can deduct them only as a miscellaneous itemized deduction, subject to the 2% of adjusted gross income limitation.

Selecting a tax advisor. Many taxpayers don't take the selection process seriously enough. Be cautious and do your homework before you choose. Remember—if your tax preparer makes a mistake or files your return late, it's *you* who will have to pay any additional taxes, penalties, and interest.

Your goal is to find someone who will charge you a fair fee, not do anything that will cause an audit, and be genuinely interested in maximizing your tax savings. Ask someone you trust whose tax situation might be similar to yours for recommendations, but don't rely on this alone. Do some investigating yourself, check references, and, above all, ask questions.

Before committing yourself, arrange brief get-acquainted meetings with several advisors and ask questions such as the following:

• What are your areas of tax specialization?
• How do you keep up to date on tax matters?
• What continuing tax education have you undertaken?
• What is your previous tax experience?

Make sure you feel comfortable with the person, but be patient—creating a good working relationship can take some time.

If you have difficulty finding a competent professional, contact the American Institute of Certified Public Accountants in New York City or the National Association of Enrolled Agents. They can supply you with names of members in good standing in your immediate area.

Some common pitfalls to avoid include retaining anyone who guarantees you a refund or who urges you to claim deductions to which you know you're not entitled, and hiring anyone whose fee is based on the amount of your refund.

Working with a professional. It's important not to just dump your tax records on your tax preparer's desk and have the preparer organize them for you. It will cost you money in increased fees. For best results, follow these guidelines:

• Present all your records in an orderly manner, categorized and summarized.
• Ask about hourly rates and other expenses of people working on your return, and find out how you might help minimize fees.
• Meet the staff people working on your return.
• Ask to receive copies of any correspondence related to you and ask for explanations for each claimed amount you don't understand.
• Before you sign your return, read each line carefully and compare the figures to your own wherever possible. And *never* sign an incomplete return.

133

- Make sure the tax preparer signs the return that is filed and that you receive a copy.
- If you're being audited, discuss with your tax advisor beforehand how much of each deduction under review may be allowed. Then you'll know when to be flexible and when to be firm with the IRS. (For more information on preparing for an audit, see page 136.)
- During the year, consult your advisor about any financial move you're contemplating that may have tax implications.

Preparers' penalties and other rules. According to the IRS code, tax return preparers are subject to criminal penalties if they make an unauthorized disclosure of tax return information or use such information for any purpose other than to prepare a return. There are also penalties for understatement of taxpayer liability. And penalties are assessable for failing to meet the following requirements, unless the failure is due to reasonable cause and not to willful neglect:

1. The return must be signed by the person primarily responsible for preparing the return and must also indicate the preparer's and/or firm's identification number.

2. At the time the return is presented for signing, the taxpayer must be provided with a completed copy of the final return, though this copy need not be signed by the preparer.

3. For three years, preparers must keep available for IRS inspection a record of the name, taxpayer identification number, and principal place of work of each tax preparer who worked for them during the period.

4. Preparers required to sign returns must advise taxpayers of the substantiation requirements of Section 274(d) of the code related to travel and entertainment expenses, business gifts, and certain depreciation deductions. Preparers should receive assurances that such substantiation exists, but it need not be in writing.

These and other legal requirements have been established by Congress to protect the public against incompetent and dishonest tax preparers. Your awareness of these requirements can help you protect yourself. ■

Most taxpayers' contact with the IRS is minimal—they file their return and pay their tax or receive a refund, whichever applies. But subsequently, some taxpayers learn that their return has been selected for an audit for any one of a number of reasons. The information that follows explains how to file and amend a return, as well as how to handle an audit.

Filing & Amending Your Return

Often, the procedures for filing a return and amending a previously filed return are not well known. Here is some information that may help you.

Filing your return. Always be sure to fill out your return completely, sign it, and file it on time. There are penalties both for late filing and nonpayment, so even if you can't pay on time, at least be sure to send in your return by the deadline.

If you can't make the filing deadline, you can get an automatic 4-month extension by filing Form 4868 and an additional 2-month extension if you have an acceptable reason. You'll be asked to estimate and pay the tax due when filing the extension. If you can't pay the full tax that's due, the IRS may, under certain circumstances, accept an installment payment plan; you'll need to agree to a monthly payment plan. Interest will be charged on amounts not paid by the due date.

Filing penalties generally don't apply if you're entitled to a refund, unless you're audited later and found to owe tax. Also, penalties for late payment can be waived if you have reasonable cause for not paying your tax when due.

Filing an amended return. Whenever you feel the tax you paid, whether resulting from an audit or some other reason, is excessive or incorrect, you have the right to file a claim for a refund. Check first, however, to be sure that no previous form you signed precludes you from filing such a claim. Individual taxpayers should use Form 1040X to file their claims. If you're amending a return for a prior year, you'll need to attach a copy of the original return.

You must file an amended return within 3 years of filing the original return or within 2 years from the date you paid any tax, whichever is later. (If you filed earlier than the due date, it's considered as filed on the due date.)

For additional information, ask the IRS for Publication 910: *Taxpayer's Guide to IRS Information, Assistance, and Publications* and Publication 586A: *The Collection Process (Income Tax Accounts).*

The Audit & Appeals Process

The job the IRS performs the year around in issuing regulations and tax forms, collecting tax returns and payments, auditing the results, and sending out refunds is indeed awesome. Often, the job is done efficiently and rapidly. But some taxpayers have found just the reverse to be true. Repetitive audits, computer breakdowns, demands for taxes not owed, and misinformation are just some of the complaints taxpayers have made about the IRS. If you experience such problems, call your local IRS office to find out where you should write.

What you need to learn from this is not to feel threatened if you're being audited. As long as you have tax knowledge, good records, and the necessary documentation, you can feel perfectly confident when questioned. The IRS is much less likely to spend audit time on you than on someone with poor records or no records at all.

How returns are selected for audit. Most taxpayers never get audited. Don't think that just because you *are* selected you're suspected of being dishonest. Also don't think that because you received your refund or filed during the last-minute rush you won't be audited. A look at the information below will help explain the selection process.

1. The majority of all selected returns (approximately 75%) come from a computer program called Discriminant Function System (DIF), which attaches a certain score to every line on your return. The computer compares your return with averages of other taxpayers and attaches a line-by-line score. The higher your score above a predetermined minimum, the more likely you are to be selected.

2. The Taxpayer Compliance Measurement Program (TCMP) is a totally random-sample

selection process. The sample for the entire nation is small (about 50,000), but you might call it the unlucky lottery system. It's a time-consuming examination where you'll be expected to prove *every* item on your return.

3. In the matching documents method, computers match income information supplied to the IRS on forms (such as the W-2 and 1099) with information on taxpayers' returns.

4. Certain target groups, such as designated occupations and tax shelters, are selected from time to time for auditing.

5. Unusual or large amounts of income or expenses could flag your return for audit. Travel and entertainment expenses have always been a popular audit subject.

6. Tips from informants, often ex-spouses or unhappy ex-employees, can trigger audits.

7. Repetitive audits are legal as long as the previous one resulted in additional tax due. However, if the same items in a previous year resulted in no change in liability, you can probably get the audit suspended.

Tax$aver Tip. *If your return shows some unusual or large amounts that you feel*

could target it for an audit, attach proof for the amounts directly to your return, along with a narrative explanation.

Always make sure all income is declared so there will be no discrepancy between your return and information already supplied to the IRS. Generally, the IRS can audit your returns for the 3 previous years. If fraud is suspected or no return is filed, it can go back to any year.

How to prepare for an audit. The principal reasons the IRS disallows deductions are incomplete records and inadequate substantiation for claimed expenses. Provide the proof and all you'll need is a lot of patience to survive an audit. It also helps if your can communicate using IRS terms and if you understand some relevant tax law.

You'll have to decide whether to handle the audit yourself or have a qualified professional represent you. If the issues are simple and the amounts involved are small, try it alone. If not, get help (see page 132 for information on how to select a tax advisor). You should, however, compare the potential tax savings with your advisor's estimated fees. When large amounts of tax are at stake, a professional may achieve not only a quicker resolution but also a more favorable one for you.

Regardless of who deals with the IRS, here are some helpful suggestions:

1. If possible, insist that the entire matter be handled by correspondence and telephone. This allows you to stick to the issues, avoid personality conflicts, and resolve the audit more quickly.

2. If it must be in person, be familiar with your return, especially the items in question. IRS agents are under a lot of pressure to reach an agreement at the first meeting, so use this to your advantage by bringing with you everything you might possibly need to prove each item.

3. If the item in question is in a gray area of the law, be aggressive, especially if your records are complete. Argue that you're supplying exactly what the law requires.

4. Don't evade or conceal information—this can result in a full-scale audit of your entire return.

5. With prior approval, you can tape-record all meetings, and so can the IRS.

6. And now for the don'ts. Don't try to be friends with the agent or, conversely, get angry. Don't volunteer any information—just answer the questions. And don't sign anything until you've had a lot of time to review it (with professional help), because once you sign a consent form, there's no appeal.

If you and the examining agent don't agree, ask to see the agent's supervisor, who may be easier to deal with in trying to reach a final agreement.

The appeals process. The IRS has established an elaborate system of appeals which offers you a wide variety of options. If you didn't reach an agreement with the agent's supervisor, your next stop, and the only one still within the IRS, is the Appeals Office in your region. It's very informal—you can represent yourself if you like—and most audits are resolved at this level. Because the appeals officer can bargain with you, be aware that negotiation will be a constant activity from this point forward. There can be good-faith settlement offers and counteroffers by both sides.

The higher the authority, the more likely the compromise—the IRS wants to settle as much as you do. Keep in mind that at any stage of the appeal procedure you can do any of the following:

1. Agree and arrange to pay the tax.
2. Ask the IRS to send you a notice of deficiency in order for you to file a petition with the Tax Court.
3. Pay the tax and immediately file a claim for a refund.

For more information, ask your local IRS office for Publication 556: *Examination of Returns, Appeal Rights, and Claims for Refund.*

The court system. More and more taxpayers are settling disputes with the IRS through litigation. The number of new cases has significantly increased in recent years, resulting in a large backlog.

The Tax Court will hear your case only if the disputed tax has not been assessed or paid. If it has been paid and you've filed for a refund, you must file suit either in the U.S. District Court or the U.S. Court of Claims. You may represent yourself (about half the taxpayers do) or have an attorney or someone else admitted to practice before that court represent you. You should know that most cases filed in Tax Court are settled out of court.

Tax$aver Tip. *If the dispute involves $10,000 or less (including taxes and penalties) for any one tax year, you can have it handled as a "small tax case." The advantages are that you can represent yourself, a final binding decision can be rendered with a minimum of expense and delay, trial judges have much latitude as to the rules of evidence, and the proceedings are simple and informal.*

No formal written opinion is issued, and the decision can't be used as a precedent by other taxpayers. But you give up your right to appeal if the decision goes against you. For a petition form and other information, write to the Clerk of the Court, U.S. Tax Court, 400 Second Street, NW, Washington, D.C. 20217. ∎

Glossary of IRS Terms

Accelerated cost recovery system (ACRS): A system of depreciating most business assets that's required for all assets placed in service after 1980; requires use of defined time periods and percentages. Modified ACRS (MACRS) is used for assets subject to the provisions of the Tax Reform Act of 1986.

Accrual basis method: A method of reporting income when earned (not received) and deducting expenses when incurred (not when paid).

Actual cost method (ACM): A method for claiming automobile operating costs that requires detailed records of each item of expense, including depreciation.

Adjusted gross income (AGI): Gross income from all sources reduced by certain allowable deductions and losses (but not itemized deductions).

Associated with test: Requirement that entertainment expenses be associated with the active conduct of a trade or business in order to be deductible; a clear business purpose in making the expenditure must be established, and the expenditure must be ordinary and necessary.

Away from home: Any period of time longer than an ordinary work day which includes time for sleep and rest.

Business associate: Any person with whom a taxpayer could reasonably expect to engage or deal in the active conduct of a trade or business; includes customers, clients, suppliers, employees, agents, partners, and professional advisors, whether established or prospective.

Business entertainment: Any trade- or business-connected activity generally considered to constitute entertainment; also recreation and amusement activities.

Business relationship test: Requirement that there be a proximate relationship to business.

Business use percentage (BUP): A percentage determined by dividing business use (either in square footage, miles, or time) by total square footage, miles, or time available for all uses.

Cash basis method: A method of reporting income when received and deducting expenses when paid.

Constructive receipt: Having the right to draw on income, even if that income is not physically in a taxpayer's possession; such income is taxable only for cash basis taxpayers.

Convenience of employer test: This test is satisfied if an employer requires an employee to use something, such as a car, as a condition of employment in order to properly perform the employee's duties.

Depreciation: The systematic allocation of the cost of an asset over some period of time by various methods.

Directly related test: Entertainment is considered directly related to business only when all the following requirements are satisfied:

1. At the time, the taxpayer had more than a *general expectation* of deriving income or other business benefit at some future date (not merely goodwill). Income or benefit does not have to result from each expenditure.

2. During the entertainment period, the taxpayer was *actively engaged* in a business meeting, discussion, or transaction with the person(s) being entertained.

3. The principal purpose of the entertainment was business.

4. The money spent was allocable to the person(s) with whom the taxpayer engaged in the active conduct of trade or business during the entertainment.

Employee: Someone subject to the will and control of an employer, not only as to what shall be done but also as to how and when it shall be done.

Exclusive use test: This test is satisfied if the portion of the home being used for business purposes is not used for any other purpose at any time during the taxable year.

Indefinite assignment: An assignment where the end cannot be foreseen within a fixed and reasonably short period of time.

Independent contractor: Someone responsible only for the result of the work to be done, not the means and methods of doing so.

Listed property: Depreciable business property used as a means of transportation; any property of a type generally used for purposes of entertainment, recreation, or amusement; and any other property specified by the regulations and purchased or leased and placed in service after June 18, 1984.

Local transportation expenses: The cost to get from one point to another, as differentiated from "travel expenses," which include meals and lodging while away from home.

Ordinary and necessary: An expenditure is *ordinary* if it is a common and accepted practice in a particular trade or business; to be *necessary*, it should be appropriate and helpful in the performance, promotion, or furtherance of a trade or business.

Per diem allowance: A fixed amount of money allowed by an employer for daily away-from-home expenses, such as meals, lodging, laundry, cleaning, and tips.

Placed in service: The date property is in a condition or state of readiness and is available for a specifically assigned use.

Principal place of business: The primary location for conducting business, determined by income earned, time spent, and facilities available.

Recapture rule: When tax benefits claimed under certain rules for depreciation and investment tax credit have to be paid back because of something that occurs in a later year, such as an early disposition of the asset or failure to meet the BUP 50% test.

Section 179 deduction: An election that allows a taypayer to write off the entire cost (up to $10,000) of an asset the year it's placed in service, subject to income limitations.

Self-employment tax: A substitute social security tax for individuals who are in business for themselves.

Standard mileage rate (SMR): An amount allowed for automobile operating costs, currently 22½¢ per mile for the first 15,000 miles and 11¢ per mile for additional mileage and for fully depreciated cars.

Straight-line depreciation: A method of deducting the cost of an asset equally each year over its estimated useful life.

Substantial business discussion: A business meeting, negotiation, discussion, or transaction which, when combined with entertainment, is for the purpose of deriving income or other specific business benefits. It is not necessary that more time be devoted to business than to entertainment to meet this test.

Tax home: Main place of business, regardless of where the family home is located; entire city or area where business is located.

Temporary assignment: An assignment where the end can be estimated within a fixed and reasonably short period of time.

Index

Sunset Proof-of-Purchase
ISBN 0-376-07027-7